PORTUGUESE STUDIES

Volume 37 Number 2
2021

Literatures and Cultures of the Indian Ocean

Guest Editors
Ana Mafalda Leite
Elena Brugioni
Jessica Falconi

Founding Editor
Helder Macedo

Editors
Jane-Marie Collins
Catarina Fouto
Tori Holmes
Paulo de Medeiros
Hilary Owen
Emanuelle Santos
Maria Tavares
Claire Williams

Editorial Assistant
Richard Correll

Production Editor
Graham Nelson

MODERN HUMANITIES RESEARCH ASSOCIATION

PORTUGUESE STUDIES

A peer-reviewed biannual multi-disciplinary journal devoted to research on the cultures, literatures, history and societies of the Lusophone world

International Advisory Board

David Brookshaw
João de Pina Cabral
Ivo José de Castro
Thomas F. Earle
John Gledson
Anna Klobucka

Maria Manuel Lisboa
Kenneth Maxwell
Laura de Mello e Souza
Maria Irene Ramalho
Silviano Santiago

Portuguese Studies and other journals published by the MHRA may be ordered from Turpin Distribution (http://ebiz.turpin-distribution.com/).

The **Modern Humanities Research Association** was founded in Cambridge in 1918 and has become an international organization with members in all parts of the world. It is a registered charity number 1064670, and a company limited by guarantee, registered in England number 3446016. Its main object is to encourage advanced study and research in modern and medieval European languages, literatures, and cultures by its publication of journals, book series, and its Style Guide. Further information about the activities of the Association and individual membership may be obtained from the Membership Secretary, email membership@mhra.org.uk, or from the website at: www.mhra.org.uk

Disclaimer: Statements of fact and opinion in the content of *Portuguese Studies* are those of the respective authors and contributors and not of the journal editors or of the Modern Humanities Research Association (MHRA). MHRA makes no representation, express or implied, in respect of the accuracy of the material in this journal and cannot accept any legal responsibility or liability for any errors or omissions that may be made.

Parts of this work may be reproduced as permitted under legal provisions for fair dealing (or fair use) for the purposes of research, private study, criticism, or review, or when a relevant collective licensing agreement is in place. All other reproduction requires the written permission of the copyright holder who may be contacted at rights@mhra.org.uk.

ISSN 0267–5315 (print) ISSN 2222–4270 (online)
ISBN 978-1-78188-610-6

© 2021 The Modern Humanities Research Association
Salisbury House, Station Road, Cambridge CB1 2LA, United Kingdom

Portuguese Studies vol. 37 no. 2

Literatures and Cultures of the Indian Ocean

CONTENTS

Obituary for Robin Warner Carmen Ramos Villar	147
Introduction Ana Mafalda Leite, Elena Brugioni and Jessica Falconi	149
The Indian Ocean as a Transnational Critical and Aesthetic Paradigm: A Study on Mozambican Literature — João Paulo Borges Coelho and Rui Knopfli Ana Mafalda Leite and Elena Brugioni	153
Islands, Theory and the Postcolonial Environment: Reading the Work of Khal Torabully Elena Brugioni and Ute Fendler	165
Combining the Uneven: Literatures of the Lusophone Indian Ocean in the Context of World-Literature — Proposal for a Theoretical Approach Applied to Mozambican Literature Marta Banasiak	178
Literature in Transit between Goa and Mozambique: Campos Oliveira as a Pioneer Figure Ana Mafalda Leite and Joana Passos	193
The Other (Hi)Stories: Diasporic Tides of the (Lusophone) Indian Ocean in *Skin* and *O Outro Pé da Sereia* Kamila Krakowska Rodrigues	210
Enchanted Things to Narrate the Oceans: João Paulo Borges Coelho and Luís Cardoso Jessica Falconi	224
East Timorese Literary Narratives (Twenty-First Century): Indian Ocean Crossings and Littoral Encounters Giulia Spinuzza	242
Reviews	256
Abstracts	269

NOTES FOR CONTRIBUTORS

Articles to be considered for publication may be on any subject within the field but must not exceed 7,500 words, and should be submitted in a form ready for publication in English, sent as an email attachment to the Editorial Assistant at portuguese@mhra.org.uk.

Contributions whose standard of English is inadequate will be returned. Any quotations in Portuguese must be accompanied by an English translation. Submissions in Portuguese may be considered, but full peer review and publication will be conditional on provision of a satisfactory translation by or on behalf of the author. The Editorial Assistant may undertake translations on request for a reasonable charge.

Text and references should conform precisely to the conventions of the *MHRA Style Guide*, 3rd edn, 2013 (978-1-78188-009-8), £9.50, $19.00, €12.00, obtainable in print or online version from www.style.mhra.org.uk. All articles are subject to independent, anonymous peer review by experts in the field; authors receive written feedback on the editors' decision and guidance on any revisions required. *Portuguese Studies* regrets it must charge contributors for the cost of corrections in proof deemed excessive.

It is a condition of publication in this journal that authors of articles and reviews assign copyright, including electronic copyright, to the MHRA. Inter alia, this allows the General Editor to deal efficiently and consistently with requests from third parties for permission to reproduce material. The journal has been published simultaneously in printed and electronic form since January 2001. Permission, without fee, for authors to use their own material in other publications, after a reasonable period of time has elapsed, is not normally withheld. Authors may make closed-access deposit of accepted manuscripts in their academic institution's digital repository upon acceptance. Full open access to the accepted manuscript is permitted no sooner than 12 months following publication of the Contribution by the MHRA. Contributions may also be republished on authors' personal websites without seeking further permission from the Association, but no earlier than 12 months after publication by the MHRA.

Books for review should be sent to: Reviews Editor, *Portuguese Studies*, Dr Emanuelle Santos, Ashley Building, Department of Modern Languages, University of Birmingham, Edgbaston, Birmingham B15 2TT, email e.santos@bham.ac.uk.

Obituary
Robin Warner (1940–2021)

CARMEN RAMOS VILLAR

University of Sheffield

The evening of the 11 August 2021 brought the very sad news that Robin Warner had passed away at the Broomgrove Nursing Home, in Sheffield, after being diagnosed with a recurrence of the lung cancer for which he had been treated some years earlier. Robin, a Senior Lecturer in Hispanic Studies at the University of Sheffield, worked for forty years in our department teaching Spanish and Portuguese Studies, and was instrumental in the promotion and growth of Portuguese as a discipline at Sheffield. Robin leaves behind an understated legacy, both in the academic and personal sense.

As a Hispanist, his publications were wide-ranging, including subjects such as Spanish theatre, Spanish and Portuguese poetry, Hispanic cartoons, Spanish and Portuguese linguistics, Spanish and Portuguese approaches to translation, and Brazilian music. His lively English translation, with Dominic Keown, of Ramón del Valle Inclán's *Esperpento de los Cuernos de Don Friolera* [*The Grotesque Farce of Mr Punch the Cuckold*] (Liverpool University Press; Aris and Phillips Hispanic Classics, 1991), remains an entertaining and classic rendition. The breadth of his academic outputs reflected his intellectually curious thirst for knowledge — he was interested in the challenge of finding out, in piecing things together, and this made him a fascinating person to talk to about anything. He would often just drop an observation into the conversation in his wish to know more, bringing in a fresh perspective on the subject or just words of encouragement.

For many years, he was instrumental in promoting and sustaining the study of Portuguese at the University of Sheffield. Generations of students and tutors passed through his hands there, and many have shared fond memories of him since they learned the news of his death. For me, he was instrumental in creating my post, one wholly dedicated to Portuguese Studies, seeing the potential to make Sheffield a centre for Portuguese Studies. In my first year, I shadowed Robin, learning the ropes from him before he retired and seeing his unique organizational skills. He welcomed me and made sure I was comfortable and ready to take over and make his vision possible. I had the privilege of observing him teach. His classes were models of challenge, stretching people just far enough, but with friendly helpful hints so that no one was left behind. I can remember him bringing problems from bridge games to translate into both Spanish and Portuguese in class, getting students to work through particular linguistic areas that he wanted to explore, and then seeing students just being carried along by his enthusiasm as they learned the intricacies of both languages. His homework instructions were given with just sufficient detail and guidance that the answers were almost there for those who had paid attention. He wanted people to thrive, to show what they could do. He did not want to catch them out, and this was the important lesson I learned from him as a teacher. It was an innate kindness that made him a lovely colleague — and a hard act to follow.

For me, Robin was a friend who was generous, gentle, kind and funny, and had one of the sharpest minds I have ever met. I don't think I can once remember him getting angry or upset. I remember him as a storyteller, and as the subject, himself, of many stories involving the most unlikely places where he had misplaced or lost his keys. The stories he would personally tell often centred on him accidentally doing or experiencing something, ranging from something he had just read, to something that had happened to him, or something he had become interested in. These stories would always be brought to an end with a very funny observation, which he would deliver rocking back and forth as he giggled. This is how I remember him, happy, putting himself in the background, helping others, being kind. When he did a pioneering stint as the Chair of ACIS (Association for Contemporary Iberian Studies) in the late 1990s, the first Lusitanist to be honoured with this office, he was tireless in supporting the organizers of the annual conference at Coimbra University, in 1997 (the first time the Association had gone to Portugal) and in ensuring that all the delegates enjoyed a memorable occasion.

That was Robin the academic and the academic colleague, but there are other sides to him too — the keen walker, the bridge player, the hero that prevented a donkey from being stolen during his year abroad... and this is just scratching the surface of his interesting life. Only at his funeral did I find out that Robin had come from a working-class Leicester background, and had been the first person in the family to go as far as he did with his studies. As people shared their stories about Robin, the common theme was that he always put others first, wanting to hear their stories, their ideas, and just spend time having a nice chat, quietly supporting people so that they could be the ones to shine. His legacy, then, lies in his desire to pass on the opportunities he had. And this is surely Robin's most lasting gift, reflected in the many lives he touched and changed as a result of having known him.

Introduction

Ana Mafalda Leite,
Elena Brugioni and Jessica Falconi

The present volume results from the scholarly work conducted by members of the research project NILUS — Narratives of the Indian Ocean in the Lusophone Space.[1] The main purpose of the project consisted in establishing a theoretical and disciplinary connection between Lusophone Literary, Visual and Cultural Studies and the transdisciplinary field of Indian Ocean Studies. The project focused on the written and visual narratives hailing from, or related to, the territories formerly colonized by Portugal along the Indian Ocean, specifically Mozambique, Goa, and East Timor.[2] This volume, therefore, constitutes an attempt to bridge a significant critical and disciplinary gap, motivated by an almost total lack of dialogue among the above-mentioned fields of study.[3] This lack of dialogue becomes ever more apparent if we bear in mind the increasingly central role played by historical, anthropological, literary, and cultural studies of the Atlantic Ocean in addressing colonial and postcolonial cultural and identity-related outputs and relations from the territories that came out of Portuguese colonial rule. Consider, for instance, the influence of the notion of Brown Atlantic (Atlântico Pardo), developed by the anthropologist Miguel Vale de Almeida as a counterpoint to Paul Gilroy's Black Atlantic, or the use of the Portugal-Brazil-Angola triangulation in comparative and transnational-oriented literary and cultural studies.[4]

While developing this disciplinary and critical dialogue to understand how the Indian Ocean and the former Portuguese colonies interact, illuminating each other in colonial and post-colonial cultural and literary outputs, we have encountered several challenges. Mainly, such challenges stem from the need to give voice to the historical and cultural specificities of the spaces under consideration, conveyed and mediated by the featured narratives; and to integrate these narratives into wider categories, approaching them from angles

---

[1] The NILUS project (PTDC/CPC-ELT/4868/2014) was funded by the Portuguese Foundation for Science and Technology and coordinated by Ana Mafalda Leite at CEsA — Center for African and Development Studies of the Lisbon School of Economics and Management, University of Lisbon.
[2] Further details concerning the aims, methods and results of the Project can be found here: <https://cesa.rc.iseg.ulisboa.pt/nilus/projeto/> [accessed on 14 October 2021].
[3] In this respect, see the anthologies of theoretical texts published by project NILUS: Ana Mafalda Leite, Elena Brugioni and Jessica Falconi (eds), *Estudos sobre o Oceano Índico: antologia de textos teóricos (excertos)* (Lisbon: CESA-ISEG, 2020), eBook: <http://hdl.handle.net/10400.5/19965>; and Ana Mafalda Leite, Elena Brugioni and Jessica Falconi (eds), *Estudos sobre o Oceano Índico: antologia de textos teóricos* (Lisbon: Colibri, 2019).
[4] On this topic, see: Ana Mafalda Leite, Jessica Falconi and Elena Brugioni (eds), 'Espaços transnacionais: narrativas do Oceano Índico', *Remate de males*, 38.1 (2018), E-ISSN 2316-5758.

that emphasize the undeniable presence of this ocean, as a reference and as a multifaceted archive — historical, cultural, material, and aesthetic.

Thus, the NILUS project aimed not only at identifying and applying concepts and tools from the field of Indian Ocean Studies to the analysis of these narratives — which did prove productive — but also at investigating peculiar and minor declensions[5] of those aspects thought to characterize the political, economic, and cultural system of the Indian Ocean, such as circulation, migration, diaspora, material culture, among others. So far, these declensions have remained largely unexplored by 'Lusophone' literary studies and by the literary strand of Indian Ocean Studies. In the latter context, the literary productions from the territories focused on by the NILUS project suffer from the inequalities of the global literary system, according to what Paulo de Medeiros, referring to postcolonial literatures in Portuguese, defines as 'redoubled forms of invisibility'.[6] Which perspectives and voices can be observed and deciphered through the lens of Indian Ocean Studies? How can this field of study, in connection with Lusophone regional and national contexts, offer critical and analytical possibilities that would otherwise remain untapped? These were some of the questions that project NILUS attempted to answer — albeit partially — and that this volume endeavours to present.

We believe that the articles gathered in this volume offer an account of the research conducted on peculiar and minor declensions of the defining features of the Indian Ocean universe, as they deal with diversified texts and writing genres — short stories, poems, chronicles, novels — and cover a time span that ranges from the nineteenth century to the present day. Moreover, the articles represent a corpus of authors which, despite being small-scale, includes well-known and emerging names, such as João Paulo Borges Coelho, Rui Knopfli, Mia Couto, Campos Oliveira, Sérgio Raimundo, Luís Cardoso, and Margaret Mascarenhas. If an Indian Ocean-based approach to the work of an author such as Mia Couto (see the article by Krakowska Rodrigues) further develops and reinforces a critical stance already observed in comparative studies,[7] partly thanks to the international circulation and reception of his work, then we believe it is necessary to underscore the importance of authors such as João Paulo Borges Coelho and Luís Cardoso for studying the oceanic dimension of contemporary narratives in Portuguese — one that simultaneously surpasses and illuminates the established national dimension in manifold ways. In particular,

---

[5] This term is a creative derivative of the grammatical concept of 'inflection'. It conveys the notion of change as it occurs in certain contexts and narratives but which can nonetheless be traced to a theoretical and geographical common root.

[6] Paulo de Medeiros, 'Mia Couto and the Antinomies of World-Literature', in *The Worlds of Mia Couto*, ed. by Kristian van Haesendonck (Oxford: Peter Lang, 2020), pp. 11–31.

[7] See, among others, David Brookshaw, 'Indianos e o Índico: o pós-colonialismo transoceânico e internacional em *O outro pé da sereia* de Mia Couto', in *Moçambique: das palavras escritas*, ed. by Margarida Calafate Ribeiro and Maria Paula Meneses (Porto: Afrontamento, 2008), pp. 129–39; and Meg Samuelson, 'Coastal Form: Amphibian Positions, Wider Worlds, and Planetary Horizons on the African Indian Ocean Littoral', *Comparative Literature*, 69.1 (2017), 16–24.

we draw the reader's attention to the short story 'The Enchanted Cloth' from João Paulo Borges Coelho's collection titled *Índicos Indícios* (addressed in the articles by Leite & Brugioni, and Falconi) and the novel *Requiem for the Solitary Sailor* by Luís Cardoso (see the articles by Falconi and Spinuzza). The characters in these texts are built and interact within relationships of solidarity, cooperation, conflict, and contradiction, questioning crystalized notions of belonging that are exclusively territorial. Hence, they epitomize the human and material dimension of the Indian Ocean. We further believe that the figure of Campos Oliveira and his role in the development of print culture between different margins of the Indian Ocean represent a potential Indo-Oceanic declension of the 'itinerant quality of Portuguese colonialism'.[8] As yet, this possibility has been sparsely explored vis-à-vis the colonial literary trajectories in the area and is therefore likely to offer a more consistent strand of research in this context.

In a similar vein, the inclusion of Fendler and Brugioni's article about the poetic production and conceptual elaboration of Khal Torabully follows from the need to consider other views on the cultural identities marked by the history and materiality of the Indian Ocean, with less circulation and academic recognition in comparison to theorizations originating from the Atlantic. In fact, the coral identity's conceptual focus on processes of agglutination, combination and ceaseless negotiation among different elements, rather than on fusion and hybridization, holds potential for investigating literary outputs from contexts which are historically marked by the hegemonic narrative of Lusotropicalism, even if they do not fit socially or culturally into the categories of creoleness and creolization as they have come to be defined in the frame of Portuguese colonization and colonialism.

We would further like to stress that the analyses conducted as part of the NILUS project revolve around three main topic clusters, which, in general, also surface in the articles herein compiled: the representation of space, the representation of peoples, and the representation of material culture. These topic clusters intertwine throughout the narratives analysed in this volume and have been deliberately explored to accentuate the island, coastal or maritime dimension, in addition to the oceanic interconnections that make for a multifaceted, and at times contrasting, imagery of the Indian Ocean and of the territories that line its shores, in keeping with the complicating nature of this ocean, as noted by Isabel Hofmeyr.[9]

The insular areas featured in the narratives selected for the analysis — the small Island of Mozambique, the Island of Timor, and the Island of Mauritius — come forth in the articles in their many declensions, that is, as coastal

---

[8] Pamila Gupta, *Portuguese Decolonization in the Indian Ocean World* (London: Bloomsbury Academic, 2017), p. 11.
[9] Isabel Hofmeyr, 'The Complicating Sea: The Indian Ocean as Method', *Comparative Studies of South Asia, Africa and the Middle East*, 32.3 (2012), 584–90.

heterotopias or societies, minor and complex places of cosmopolitanism and transnationalism, often absent from colonial and postcolonial hegemonic cartographies. In either case, those areas emerge as privileged locations for reflection about cultural and material transit, about local, national and transnational identities, as well as individual intellectual itineraries and collective historical trajectories, shedding light, if only partially, on peculiar aspects and configurations of Indian Ocean literatures and cultures.

The Indian Ocean as a Transnational Critical and Aesthetic Paradigm: A Study on Mozambican Literature — João Paulo Borges Coelho and Rui Knopfli

ANA MAFALDA LEITE and ELENA BRUGIONI

University of Lisbon/CEsA / University of Campinas (UNICAMP)

Amongst the essential bibliography of Indian Ocean Studies[1] there are a significant number of specific disciplinary and diachronic perspectives, which could be defined as a set of hegemonic perspectives in competition. As regards the disciplinary dimension, historically oriented literary production, in its political and anthropological interrelations, is noticeably more widely and deeply developed. With reference to the diachronic dimension, there is an evident prevalence of approaches focused on the pre-modern age while the modern and contemporary periods remain uncharted.[2] In an attempt to achieve a deeper (even if concise) understanding of the conceptual and epistemological dimension of this field of study, one might point out — along the lines of the reflection proposed by Fernand Braudel and viewing the sea as a venue of historical, economic and cultural relationships[3] — that Indian Ocean Studies [IOS] provides various epistemological itineraries which portray the Indian Ocean as an 'inter-regional arena';[4] one which could be the stage of new subjects, relationships, and specific, as well as alternative, representations that conceptually match what Michel Foucault defines as 'heterotopia':

---

[1] For a first bibliographical approach to Indian Ocean Studies, within a vast and diversified critical production, see Shanty Moorthy and Ashraf Jamal (eds), *Indian Ocean Studies: Cultural, Social, and Political Perspectives* (London and New York: Routledge, 2010); Sugata Bose, *A Hundred Horizons: The Indian Ocean in an Age of Global Empire* (Cambridge, MA: Harvard University Press, 2006); Gwyn Campbell (ed.), *The Structure of Slavery in Indian Ocean Africa and Asia* (London: Frank Cass, 2004); Milo Kearney, *The Indian Ocean in World History* (London: Routledge, 2004); Leila Tarazi Fawaz et al. (eds), *Modernity and Culture: From the Mediterranean to the Indian Ocean* (New York: Columbia University Press, 2002); Michael N. Pearson, *The Indian Ocean* (London: Routledge, 2003); Michael N. Pearson, *Port Cities and Intruders: The Swahili Coast, India and Portugal in the Early Modern Era* (Baltimore, MD: Johns Hopkins University Press, 1998); Kenneth McPhearson, *The Indian Ocean: A History of People and the Sea* (Delhi: Oxford University Press, 1993); Françoise Vergès, 'Writing on Water: Peripheries, Flows, Capital, and Struggles in the Indian Ocean', *Positions: East Asia Cultures Critique*, special issue, The Afro-Asian Century, 11.1 (2003), 241–57.
[2] On this aspect see Michael N. Pearson, 'History of the Indian Ocean: A Review Essay', *WASAFIRI*, 26.2 (2011), 78–99.
[3] Fernand Braudel, *La Méditerranée*, vol. I: *L'Espace et l'Histoire*; vol. II: *Les Hommes et l'Héritage* (Paris: Flammarion, 1985).
[4] Bose, *A Hundred Horizons*, p. 6.

> First there are the utopias. Utopias are sites with no real place. They are sites that have a general relation of direct or inverted analogy with the real space of Society. They present society itself in a perfected form, or else society turned upside down, but in any case these utopias are fundamentally unreal spaces.
> There are also, probably in every culture, in every civilization, real places — places that do exist and that are formed in the very founding of society — which are something like counter-sites, a kind of effectively enacted utopia in which the real sites, all the other real sites that can be found within the culture, are simultaneously represented, contested, and inverted. Places of this kind are outside of all places, even though it may be possible to indicate their location in reality. Because these places are absolutely different from all the sites that they reflect and speak about, I shall call them, by way of contrast to utopias, heterotopias. I believe that between utopias and these quite other sites, these heterotopias, there might be a sort of mixed, joint experience, which would be the mirror.[5]

From a literary and cultural perspective, the definition of the Indian Ocean as a space of structured relationships[6] or even as a transnational paradigm[7] is key, as it provides a basis for reflection about the differences, ambiguities and tensions that characterize the Indian Ocean, focusing on the human dimension of this maritime space:

> To speak of a 'human ocean', then, is not merely to speak adjectivally, or metaphorically, but to harness human cultural practice to the element which has made it possible. Moreover, to think the oceanic human is also to affirm 'the rearrangement of desires' within the ethico-political sphere of the humanities.[8]

Thus, the connection between the national and regional perspectives and the human dimension — the human ocean — constitutes a particularly effective conceptual apparatus to analyse the relationship between history and narration that some authors seem to develop, portraying the Indian Ocean as a transnational critical paradigm that allows us to rethink the relationship between history, narrative and imagination. As for the so-called African Literatures, this critical and conceptual role is especially interesting as regards two central issues: on the one hand, the aesthetics of the Indian Ocean, as theme and motif in — written and visual — narratives that define and (re)present this space and its meanings as a counterpoint to the national contexts in which such proposals are embedded; on the other hand, the Indian Ocean as a transnational conceptual and analytic paradigm that points to the

---

[5] Michel Foucault, 'Of Other Spaces, Heterotopias', *Architecture, Mouvement, Continuité*, 5 (1984), 46–49.
[6] Kirti N. Chaudhuri, *Asia before Europe: Economy and Civilization of the Indian Ocean from the Rise of Islam to 1750* (Cambridge: Cambridge University Press, 1990).
[7] Isabel Hofmeyr, 'The Black Atlantic meets the Indian Ocean: Forging New Paradigms of Transnationalism for the Global South — Literary and Cultural Perspectives', *Social Dynamics: A Journal of African Studies*, 33.2, (2007), 3–32.
[8] Moorthy and Jamal, *Indian Ocean Studies*, p. 14.

existence of comparative itineraries marked by dialogues amongst a variety of writings and representations, at least in linguistic and spatial terms. This in turn fostered the emergence and consolidation of counterbalancing cartographies between contemporary African writings and further paved the way for what could be defined as Literatures of the African Indian Ocean.[9] To sum up, from a cultural and literary perspective, Indian Ocean Studies entails a number of epistemological and conceptual features of great relevance, suggesting comparative itineraries that, according to Edward W. Said, correspond to a critical gesture which is irrevocably associated with different ways of seeing and imagining the world.[10] Consequently, the Indian Ocean comes forth as a 'reconquered geography'[11] of the contemporary imagery, an aesthetic and political space freed from imperial speech, whose transnational dimension further allows us to rethink the individual and collective boundaries of the nation's space, hinting at Philip E. Steinberg's definition of 'aquatopia'.[12]

Bearing in mind the specificity of the relationship between Portugal and the Indian Ocean, in the pre-modern age and in subsequent epochs,[13] Indian Ocean Studies should represent a founding critical perspective. For that reason, it deserves a wider and more in-depth conceptual and analytical approach,[14] especially by taking into account the meaning of the Indian Ocean in what could be defined as the great Portuguese imperial narrative. In this article, we will analyse seminal texts by two Mozambican authors who deconstruct that imperial narrative, narrating the Island of Mozambique as a transnational space, where the cultures of the Orient intertwine in solidarity, as a metonymic representation of the Indian Ocean. As concerns Indian Ocean Studies in the Portuguese contemporary context, we should highlight the pioneering work organized by Rosa Maria Perez, *Culturas do Índico* [*Cultures of the Indian Ocean*][15] and also the journal *Oceanos* [*Oceans*], edited by the National

---

[9] Elena Brugioni, 'Literaturas africanas e romance histórico', in Elena Brugioni, *Literaturas africanas comparadas: paradigmas críticos e representações em contraponto* (Campinas: Editora Unicamp, 2019), pp. 19–46.
[10] Edward W. Said, *Culture and Imperialism* (New York: Vintage Books, 1993).
[11] Said, *Culture and Imperialism*.
[12] Philip E. Steinberg, *The Social Construction of the Ocean* (Cambridge: Cambridge University Press, 2001).
[13] In this regard, see some fundamental studies such as Edward A. Alpers, *East Africa and the Indian Ocean* (Princeton, NJ: Markus Wiener Publishers, 2009); Edward A. Alpers, *Ivory and Slaves: Changing Patterns of International Trade in East Africa to the Later Nineteenth Century* (Berkeley, CA: Berkeley University Press, 1975); Francisco Bethencourt and Kirti N. Chaudhuri, *História da expansão portuguesa* (Lisbon: Temas e Debates, 1998–2000); Charles R. Boxer, *Race Relations in the Portuguese Colonial Empire, 1415–1825* (Oxford: Oxford University Press, 1963); José Capela, *O tráfico de escravos nos portos de Moçambique* (Porto: Afrontamento, 2002).
[14] With regard to the Indian Ocean as a category of analysis from a literary and cultural perspective, see Mar Garcia et al. (eds), *INDICITIES/ INDICES/ INDÍCIOS: hybridations problématiques dans les littératures de l'Océan Indien* (Ille-sur-Têt: Édition K'A, 2010); Jessica Falconi, *Utopia e conflittualità: Ilha de Moçambique nella poesia mozambicana contemporanea* (Rome: Aracne, 2008); Elena Brugioni and Joana Passos (eds), Dossier 'Narrando o Índico', in *Diacrítica — Literatura*, 27.3 (2013), 7–158.
[15] Rosa Maria Perez (ed.) *Culturas do Índico* (Lisbon: Comissão Nacional para as Comemorações dos Descobrimentos Portugueses, 1998).

Commission for the Commemorations of Portuguese Discoveries between 1989 and 2002. In addition, a broad and diversified corpus of historical, anthropological, social and cultural studies has been the hallmark of scientific output about the Indian Ocean, especially when it comes to Portuguese maritime history between East Africa and Asia, during the empire and the modern age. In general, this corpus is characterized by approaches of specific national or regional contexts — Mozambique, Goa, among others — although a critical and epistemological reflection on what could be defined as an 'Indian Ocean paradigm' remains underdeveloped. Thus, anticipating the issues addressed by the theoretical reflection developed in this essay, one might argue that the Indian Ocean seems to correspond, in epistemological terms, to an 'inter-regional arena'[16] more than an 'area', or rather a 'region within a world-system';[17] however, it is worth noting that the Indian Ocean does not constitute a unitary, critical and epistemologically consolidated unit of analysis, particularly within the study of African and Mozambican literatures. At the same time, our purpose in this article is to emphasize

> [T]he vital role of the humanities as a disciplinary entry point that can prepare us for 'an "other" principle of study. [...] The ethico-political task of the humanities has always been the rearrangement of desires,' the possibility for new imaginative conjunctures.
> These conjunctures, or 'miracles of culture-contact,' could never have been possible without the seas and oceans, hence the critical shift from terrestrial to maritime cultural logics, or rather, the emergent coalescence of these perceptual modalities.[18]

Mozambique and the Indian Ocean: *Unveiling* the Archive

The Indian Ocean stands out in the works of some Mozambican authors as a symbolic and conceptual territory, where the connection between narrative, nation and history is characterized by a discontinuous and fragmentary dimension — pointing to Homi Bhabha's definition of dissemi-nation,[19] that is, an account that does not organize but merely reports on the disorientation of what is narrated and what is lived.[20] This liminal, disarticulated and fragmentary dimension which characterizes the relationship between historical narration and representation in the Indian Ocean suggests a relationship between time and narration that is not governed by the urgency of an organization of present and past time, but rather by an interrogative stance

---

[16] Bose, *A Hundred Horizons*.
[17] Moorthy and Jamal, *Indian Ocean Studies*.
[18] Moorthy and Jamal, *Indian Ocean Studies*, p. 13; citing Gayatri Chakravorty Spivak, *Other Asias* (Oxford: Blackwell Publishing, 2008).
[19] Homi K. Bhabha, 'DissemiNation: Time, Narrative, and the Margins of the Modern Nation', in Homi K. Bhabha (ed.), *Nation and Narration* (London and New York: Routledge, 1990), pp. 291–322; repr. Homi K. Bhabha, *The Location of Culture* (London and New York: Routledge, 1994), pp. 139–70.
[20] Walter Benjamin, *Sul concetto di storia* (Turin: Einaudi, 1997).

towards the past and history through the use of citation.²¹ It is mostly in the literary works of contemporary authors such as João Paulo Borges Coelho that this fragmentary configuration gains significance, providing a relevant critical framework to rethink the connection between narration, (post-)nation and community, where the Indian Ocean is viewed as a repository of 'minor histories'²² or, better still, as an archive of languages and traditions in constant reconfiguration.²³

The literary projects that João Paulo Borges Coelho has brought to the public point towards a significant redefinition of several discourses about the relationship between time and narration, history and memory, the nation and the individual,²⁴ shaping the geographic and aesthetic space of the Indian Ocean as the interstitial place whence alternative plots and subjects emerge, namely a 'third space'²⁵ of aesthetic discourses and critical paradigms that, first and foremost, aim to 'provincialize'²⁶ what has been defined as grand narratives of the empire and the nation.

In other words, the Indian Ocean and the meaning that this 'transnational imaginative geography'²⁷ seems to convey, both aesthetically and critically, become crucial to (re)signify the matrices of a larger story — imperial and national — giving back voice and place to the indices of past experiences and pointing to other stories; 'minor' ²⁸ and subjective stories that 'rescue the survivors' historical present from a pure past, devoid of living experience',²⁹ consecrating memory and experience as fundamental and (re-)founding practices to think and write 'the future of the past'.³⁰

Índicos Indícios [*Indian Indices*]³¹ is a collection of short stories divided into two volumes — *Setentrião* [*North*] and *Meridião* [*South*] — published in 2005 by João Paulo Borges Coelho.³² In this work, the author explores the relationship between Mozambique and the Indian Ocean through a set of stories which

---

²¹ Benjamin, *Sul concetto di storia*, p. 27.
²² Dipesh Chakrabarty, *Provincializing Europe: Postcolonial Thought and Historical Difference* (Princeton, NJ: Princeton University Press, 2000).
²³ Hofmeyr, 'The Black Atlantic Meets the Indian Ocean'.
²⁴ For an in-depth reflection on the literary work of Borges Coelho, and particularly on the relationships between narrative, history and memory, see Elena Brugioni, Orlando Grossegesse and Paulo de Medeiros (eds.), *A Companion to João Paulo Borges Coelho: Rewriting the (Post)Colonial Remains* (Oxford: Peter Lang, 2020).
²⁵ Bhabha, *The Location of Culture*.
²⁶ Chakrabarty, *Provincializing Europe*.
²⁷ Devleena Ghosh and Stephen Muecke (eds), *Cultures of Trade: Indian Ocean Exchanges* (Newcastle: Cambridge Scholars Publishing, 2007).
²⁸ Gill Deleuze and Felix Guattari, *Kafka, per una letteratura minore* (Macerata: Quodlibet, 1996).
²⁹ Reinhart Koselleck, *Futuro passato: per una semantica dei temi storici* (Genova: Marietti, 1996).
³⁰ Annette Wieviorka, *L'Ère du témoin* (Paris: Plon, 1998), p. 59.
³¹ All the titles of works mentioned in this essay have been translated into English upon their first occurrence.
³² João Paulo Borges Coelho, Mozambican historian and writer, is the author of a vast and differentiated literary work that focuses on the relations between history and memory in the context of Mozambique and southern Africa. His work has been translated into several languages, and in 2009 he won the Leya Award with his novel *O Olho de Hertzog* [*The Eye of Hertzog*] published in 2010 by Leya.

seem to (re)define the Mozambican physical geography and imagery, viewing the sea/ocean as a liquid archive, a repository of narratives, memories and founding traces in order to (re)signify the nation's physical and aesthetic space.

In the introduction to the volume *Setentrião*, the first of *Índicos Indícios*, João Paulo Borges Coelho adds a topographic, thematic and cultural diversity to contemporary Mozambican literature, dislocating the narrative from the predominantly southern scenery. As the author writes:

> The Indian sea bathes, one by one, the nearly two thousand five hundred kilometres of the coast of Mozambique — a significant stretch. Larger even if we consider the islands scattered along that coast — countless. And much, much larger if we bear in mind the stories that this simple fact has nurtured in the imagination of the present, and over the long period of time gone by. Calm waters that can also flare up. Blue, when the sun shines upon them, but so often brownish, tinted by any and all things the coast leaks through its liquid veins — lands and branches, memories and the drowned, plots and quests — which open unto it and fertilize it. These are Indian Indices, and I arranged them in two volumes, following a merely geographic criterion. This first one, *Setentrião*, roams the coast and the islands of the distant Mozambican north.[33]

Thus, we find ourselves in a coastal context, an-other geography, in which the sea–land duo invokes a space of convergence between the extension of the Indian sea and the shore of the land it narrativizes. And, specifically, in this combination the islands appear as special places of interweaving of the two elements and of what they represent culturally. They create, so to speak, a *topos* whose cultural rhetoric, negotiated secularly, becomes diversified. The short story 'O Pano Encantado' [The Enchanted Cloth],[34] set on the Island of Mozambique, invokes mystery, concealment, and dramatization, we might add. What lies behind the cloth? The seduction of an oriental face, whose veil conceals it? A place, a map, a sea? What is being staged here?

According to Moura,[35] the scenography of a work defines space (topography) and time (chronography), which set the tone to develop the enunciation, created by the work itself. The scenography is controlled by the literary scene which provides the work with its pragmatic (and dramatic) framework, imposing a unique discursive ritual to the performance and the representation.

To enter the Island of Mozambique you need to cross the bridge. A narrow, metallic, nearly infinite bridge that takes us from dry land to the other side. As always, there is the version of those who view the Island with strangeness, and then the version of those who consider it the centre of the world; and, on the

---

[33] João Paulo Borges Coelho, *Índicos Indícios*, I: *Setentrião* (Lisbon: Caminho, 2005), p. 9 (translations here and elsewhere are my own unless otherwise stated).

[34] The short story 'O Pano Encantado' [The Enchanted Cloth] has been translated in English by David Brookshaw and published in Elena Brugioni, Orlando Grossegesse and Paulo de Medeiros (eds), *A Companion to João Paulo Borges Coelho: Rewriting the (Post)Colonial Remains* (Oxford: Peter Lang, 2020), pp. 11–35.

[35] Jean Marc Moura, *Littératures francophones et théorie postcoloniale* (Paris: PUF, 1999), p. 120.

other side, the bush. In any case, one way or another, *it is on the bridge that all the mystery lies for, in uniting, it reminds us of separation*. Without a bridge, it would be a world apart; with it, the island turned into an island, in a closed space where you can only get in and out via the bridge. As with all islands, here too the inhabitants are restless, gazing at the continent with contempt, and at other times with longing. Never making up their minds, however, to reach for it.[36]

The bridge thus establishes the poetics of relation, to use a concept developed by Édouard Glissant,[37] and of recreation, or of transculturation, according to Fernando Ortiz,[38] since it expresses the diverse phenomena of cultures in 'contact zones', according to the definition proposed by Mary Louise Pratt.[39] Here, in this poetics of relation — in which the symbol of the bridge culturally unites and separates continent and sea, land and Indian Ocean — we consider the island as a phenomenon of an ever-changing cultural dynamics or, as Octavio Paz would put it, of signs in rotation.[40]

'O Pano Encantado' outlines several circuits: an inner and, simultaneously, an outer circuit, and others still, of memory and of a hidden history. It is a veil that opens onto the signs of orientalism,[41] not as a discourse to invent otherness, but as a strategy to disclose other subject and histories. It is also a detailed descriptive narrative of places, some of which are imagined and in imaginary reconstruction, others real and repetitively travelled. At the tailor's, the redundant route of gestures and words of the tailor and his helper; at the end of the day, the return home, passing through the bazaar, turning the corner at *Igreja da Saúde*, where Jamal, the helper, kneels for a few moments to say his prayers, and then heading home. And the narrator, bound to the character, describes in detail that other labyrinthine embroidery that the neighbourhoods make up on the path repeatedly pilgrimaged by the tailor's helper. A multiple circuit in which the short story, quite indelibly, summons former ones, in its intertextuality of descriptive narrative of the Island:

> We look at that fabric, almost banana-shaped, and we fail to see on either side anything more than the island itself. At one end, the Fortress, a rough stone skin with the soul of stark white lime; at the other end, the crematorium of the Indian traders, exuding, as a poet once said, scents and garlands, jasmine and a tall column of thick vertical smoke [...].[42]

'A poet once said' is followed by João Paulo Borges Coelho's textual reference to the poet Rui Knopfli in *A Ilha de Próspero* [*Prospero's Island*], an author who first wanders around the streets and different architectures of the Island of

---

[36] Borges Coelho, *Índicos Indícios*, I: *Setentrião*, p. 13.
[37] Édouard Glissant, *Poétique de la relation* (Paris: Gallimard, 2008).
[38] Fernando Ortiz, *Contrapunteo cubano del tabaco y azúcar* (La Habana: J. Montero, 1940).
[39] Mary Louise Pratt, *Imperial Eyes: Travel Writing and Transculturation* (London and New York: Routledge, 1992), p. 6.
[40] Octavio Paz, *Signos em rotação* (São Paulo: Editora Perspectiva, 2003).
[41] Edward W. Said, *Orientalism* (New York: Pantheon Books, 1978).
[42] Borges Coelho, *Índicos Indícios*, I: *Setentrião*, p. 43.

Mozambique when he stages and dramatizes the various cultural locations and voices of the Island.

If imperial geographic imagination led to the mapping of places and their nomination, the process of cultural reinvention and renomination of the places is a means of appropriation and reinvention of space, an itinerary which Knopfli endeavoured to accomplish in the aforementioned work and that other Mozambican poets retraced after him.[43] As Catherine Lynette Innes states:

> the trope of travel and pilgrimage is used not only to revisit the past and a consciousness which derives from the past [...]. It is striking how frequently the concept of pilgrimage becomes the framework for a reuniting of landscape and tradition in postcolonial literature.[44]

The Mozambican poet Rui Knopfli belongs to the first generation of authors to write about the Island of Mozambique, located in the far north of the country, and his writing project is still bound to a colonial context. It is a cultural space *par excellence*, in which the first poetic voice of the nineteenth century — Campos de Oliveira (1847–1911)[45] — was born, and it became the place of reference for the concept of 'cultural nation', reinventing origins other than the epic foundational gesture. Knopfli's work, at the time (1972), was especially reflective of the multifarious historical and cultural memories that surface everywhere among the architectural and religious Portuguese presence, as evidence of more remote pasts and origins preceding what is now presented as a type of circuit of the colonial presence. It is the perverse gaze of the poet — which can be read in the poem 'A Dama e o Jogral' [The Dame and the Jester]: 'enquanto dorme o castelão, penetra | o jogral humilde na alcova da princesa'. [while the castellan sleeps, the humble jester penetrates the princess's alcove][46] — that allows us to see what was erased from the colonial landscape of the island (the castellan that sleeps), but which remains, in its almost serene invisibility and contrary to colonial power, lodged in innumerable clandestine signals in that space of the Indian Ocean. This semiology of other cultures is unveiled in the 'alcove' of the poems by Knopfli the 'jester', who raises or reveals the veils of the presence of various 'orients' in the body of the Indian Ocean island.

We will consider the type of textual structure developed in Knopfli's book, in which the represented space — the Island of Mozambique, signalled poem by poem as a toured circuit (note that the term *Roteiro* [circuit] appears as a

---

[43] On the topic of the Island of Mozambique within Mozambican poetry see António Sopa and Nelson Saúte (eds), *A Ilha de Moçambique pela voz dos poetas* (Lisbon: Edições 70, 1992); Jessica Falconi, *Utopia e conflittualità: Ilha de Moçambique nella poesia mozambicana contemporanea* (Rome: Aracne, 2008) and Ana Mafalda Leite, *Cenografias pós-coloniais & estudos sobre literatura moçambicana* (Lisbon: Colibri, 2018).
[44] Catherine Lynette Innes, *The Cambridge Introduction to Postcolonial Literatures in English* (Cambridge: Cambridge University Press, 2007), p. 77.
[45] On this, see Ana Mafalda Leite, 'Tópicos para uma história da literatura moçambicana', in *Moçambique das palavras escritas*, ed. by Margarida Calafate Ribeiro and Maria Paula Meneses (Porto: Afrontamento, 2008), pp. 47–76.
[46] Rui Knopfli, *Memória Consentida: 20 Anos de Poesia 1959–1979* (Lisbon: INCM, 1982), p. 336.

subtitle to the work), or an ambulatory map — is described in twenty texts, or poetic units that align poetic narrative with the dramatization of voices, similar to a dramatic poem type. Description will be the appropriate mode of 'strategic location'[47] adopted by the author as the preferred rhetorical mode of exteriority, of space representation, through a primordial sense: the gaze. Between the act of seeing (describing exteriority) and envisioning (describing the subsequent fabling), the narrating subject, who de-scribes, will also suffer a process of multiplication (read for example the poem 'Through the Looking Glass': 'dessas imagens autónomas | em que me desdobro e multiplico' [of those autonomous images | in which I unfold and multiply]), self-dramatizing, or making room for the images/voices that emerge from the visionary act, resulting from what is beheld.

The pluralization or dissemination of the narrating subject in other utterances, other voices, is the result of this complex chronotopia, in which the visitation of the island space will be organized in a gaze, which upon seeing becomes visionary, leading to that interweaving of space and time. This in turn summons other citational dimensions, with the presence of literature, history, culture and especially of the religiosities, which, conversely, make time composite and further articulate it as a contact zone. In fact, *A Ilha de Próspero* is construed as a contact zone.[48]

In the work of Knopfli, we can observe that the poet reveals deliberate ways of addressing the reader, many times in dramatized form and staging disparate voices that inhabit the cultural body of the island; of signalling and encompassing the Indian Ocean and the Orient; of representing or speaking in its name, for which he makes use of the sacred Hindu texts and of the language that signifies them — Sanskrit; and of representing it historically with the human presence of the practically enslaved labour of the bricklayers of Diu, coming from India.

The Island of Mozambique is represented in Rui Knopfli's *A Ilha de Próspero* as a space of other imaginaries and discursive formations, alien to Prospero; as a space that shares different geographies and cultures, dominated by the presence of the Orient, as a representation of the Indian Ocean, configured and constructed citationally through reference to sacred Hindu and Islamic texts in languages such as Arabic, Urdu and Sanskrit and from the original geography of the Indian diaspora.

A Ilha de Próspero thus comprises one of the first works of Mozambican literature to open its space for reflection to the Indian Ocean through the representation of the Orient(s) that compose it, while sharing a wider regional or transnational context. Among other topics, Knopfli's book portrays the Indian Ocean based on the diverse representations of the Orient on the Island of Mozambique, questioning Prospero and the colonial power, subjugated in

---

[47] Said, *Orientalism*.
[48] Pratt, *Imperial Eyes*.

multiple ways in different poems, and especially in the last poem, 'Padrão' [Monument], where the space of the island is re-evaluated as 'porto de olvido na rota perdida das Índias' [a port of oblivion on the lost route of the Indies] that becomes 'soluço de pedra ao sabor da monção' [a hiccup of stone with the flavour of the monsoon].[49]

With its reflection on the exchange of other cultural imaginaries deriving from the Indian Ocean and incorporating different oriental representations, Knopfli's writing can be thought as 'an archive of deep and layered existing social and intellectual traditions [...]. Understanding political discourse and action, then, becomes a task of understanding a complex layered precolonial, colonial and postcolonial archive in which versions of modernity are negotiated in an ever-shifting set of idioms around tradition'.[50]

The inclusion of Knopfli's poetic account by João Paulo Borges Coelho in the short story 'O Pano Encantado', textually crystallized in the form of a palimpsest, or another archive, embroidered and enchanted, alludes to the reinvention and renomination of the Island of Mozambique as a representation of the Indian Ocean. This poetic narrative is resumed in other instances of Mozambican poetry, such as the poems by Virgílio de Lemos, Luís Carlos Patraquim or Eduardo White, among other authors. As an elemental symbol of land and sea, the Island is indeed a *topos* of renomination of several Mozambican authors; it provides an alternative to the national narrative, which entails acknowledgement and sharing of cultures from different origins. They all flow onto the Island of Mozambique and onto the islands of the Indian Ocean, which converge, rebuilt, as a result of this intermeshing, not necessarily in a state of hybridity, but rather of relationship, bridge or dialogue.

This invocation of a literary memory with different cultural journeys bears the marks of a particular form of enunciation, specifically that of travel writing and in particular the cultural circuit type, be it historical-descriptive, architectural, religious, memorialist, erotic or of literary genealogy. It is, after all, a process of unveiling; lifting the enchanted cloth [*O Pano Encantado*]; unearthing the orients therein concealed; or even of mapping anew the transcultural space of the Island of Mozambique and, metonymically, of the islands and the Indian Ocean coastline of Mozambique, as done by João Paulo Borges Coelho in the two volumes of short stories *Índicos Indícios*. As a process of historical and cultural unveiling, these different circuits create a chronotopic overlap — time-space — that reshapes the place culturally. Thus, geography becomes a form of history or vice versa, opening the possibility to (re)think the very notion of Mozambican cultural history and its entanglements within literary writing.

A similar pilgrimage in the form of embroidered, utmost secret writing

---

[49] Knopfli, *Memória Consentida*, p. 354.
[50] Hofmeyr, 'The Black Atlantic Meets the Indian Ocean', p. 13. Here we would like particularly to underline the importance of defining the Indian Ocean as a *deep, complex and layered archive*.

allows for an association between time and space, creating a unique and initiatory memory that resets and reshapes a different origin and exchange. It further allows us to trace a simultaneity of sacred and repetitive time based on the historical time of the original genealogies — that is, the time that is rhythmically set by the narrator throughout the short story, in parallel to this unveiling of the sacred maps. This time is pure, frozen, sacral, repetitive, marked, redundant, and runs on a continuous cycle:

> So slow, so light, so tenuous is time, that you can only feel it if you are truly quiet in the antechamber of numbness. It is not a breeze, because its arrival has nothing extraordinary other than the fact that it is blowing. It is time itself, and time can only be discovered if the air is immovable, if we are immovable, if the silence is complete beyond the mild trotting of the Singer that Jamal pedalled without leaving the same place.[51]

Myth and history thus intertwine in another itinerary, secret and sacred, which is drawn/embroidered in 'O Pano Encantado' and which rebuilds a sense of belonging shared not only by the Mozambican but also by Islamic, Oriental and Indian peoples. Sacredness marks the opening and integration into that kind of sacred architecture in different languages, from Swahili to English, which runs across the Indian countries in a specific poetic constellation expressing the saga of mismatch of several civilizations — Bantu, European, Arab, Javanese, Indian.

As a mythical and historical chronography of the diverse cultural legacy of the Island of Mozambique, 'O Pano Encantado' aims to bring this transnational culture into the present by recording a silenced, ignored and initiatory memory and making it a symbol of a religious culture that ramified into numerous brotherhoods, opening up to the Indian Ocean.

In the two volumes of *Índicos Indícios*, the 'human dimension of the ocean'[52] finds itself connected through spatial (from the north to the south of Mozambique) and temporal (from colonial times to the post-independence) amplitudes. These volumes fit into a conceptual perspective that regards the Indian sea/ocean as a privileged observation point or, still according to Foucault's definition, as a *heterotopia*, that is, a place of convergence between the gaze of the observer and the totality that surrounds him/her, as in Rui Knopfli's seminal poetry, enabling a redefinition of the relation between illusion (utopia) and compensation (desire).

The last trait of heterotopias is that they have a function in relation to all the space that remains. This function unfolds between two extreme poles. Either their role is to create a space of illusion that exposes every real space, all the sites inside of which human life is partitioned, as still more illusory (perhaps that is the role that was played by those famous brothels of which we are now deprived). Or else, on the contrary, their role is to create a space that is other,

---

[51] Borges Coelho, *Índicos Indícios*, I: *Setentrião*, p. 23.
[52] Moorthy and Jamal, *Indian Ocean Studies*.

another real space, as perfect, as meticulous, as well arranged as ours is messy, ill constructed, and jumbled. This latter type would be the heterotopia, not of illusion, but of compensation.[53]

In conclusion, it is worth considering some apparently distant — and yet related — circumstances that can be defined as particularly relevant within the recent history of Mozambique: on one hand, the essential role of the Indian Ocean for the position of Mozambique within the world-system (capitalistic) economy throughout the so-called maritime corridors;[54] on the other hand, the political instability determined by armed conflicts taking place in the province of Cabo Delgado, as a phenomenon also related to the Indian Ocean region.[55] Contrasting these two aspects with the ostensible absence of the Indian Ocean within the Mozambican political agenda as well as from cultural and social analysis, the relevance of addressing the sea — the Indian Ocean — in its historical, cultural and political dimension become rather significant. Therefore, *unveiling* the Indian Ocean *archive* appears to be an urgent and necessary task, possibly a fundamental gesture in order to understand and make sense of Mozambican past and present. Paraphrasing from Moorthy and Jamal, the approach we have been aiming to define is therefore archaeological:

> but not to make a fetish of the past, though there is no doubt that the relevance of the Indian Ocean region rests on an appeal to history. We aim to excavate the Indian Ocean world, both past and present, and bring to the surface a fruitful area of interdisciplinary scholarship, valuable in itself, made available through the modalities of area studies and world system analysis. Because what matters in the end is the lived human experience, and how our narratives connect in a large but small world, how to counter the gross indifference of a mediatised world with a short memory span and an amnesia for the past.[56]

---

[53] Michel Foucault, 'Of Other Spaces, Heterotopias'.
[54] On this see José Lopes, *Corredores Mineiro-Energéticos 2020: Impactos Marítimos do Afro-Índico no Canal de Moçambique* (Maputo: CESAB Centro de Estudos Sociais Aquino de Bragança, 2013) and also the publications of IESE — Instituto de Estudos Sociais e Económicos — particularly the book series *Desafios para Moçambique* and the journal Caderno IESE.
[55] On the ongoing armed attacks and violence in Cabo Delgado, among a vast bibliography, see Eric Morier-Genoud, 'A insurgência jihadi em Moçambique: origens, natureza e início', *Cadernos IESE*, 21 (2021), 1–56. The article is also available in English in *Journal of Eastern African Studies*, 14.3 (2020), 396–412.
[56] Moorthy and Jamal, *Indian Ocean Studies*, p. 19.

Islands, Theory and the Postcolonial Environment: Reading the Work of Khal Torabully[1]

ELENA BRUGIONI and UTE FENDLER

University of Campinas (UNICAMP) / University of Bayreuth

The importance of the Indian Ocean lies not only in its specificity as an area of knowledge or object of study but also in the theoretical, conceptual and epistemological renovation it entails, introducing meaningful revisions of paradigms and analytical categories that frame the field of literary and cultural studies within a postcolonial critical perspective. In these fields of study, the definition of the Indian Ocean as a space of 'structured relations',[2] as an 'interregional arena',[3] as a 'transnational paradigm',[4] or even as a 'world-system',[5] points to theoretical constellations that are both significant and original. Moreover, this definition offers food for thought on the differences, ambiguities and tensions that govern the Indian Ocean space-time, thus opening up possibilities for pertinent and innovative critical reflections and theorizations to investigate literature and its aesthetic and political meanings from a postcolonial theoretical perspective.[6] Since it would not have been possible to develop a comprehensive and detailed discussion regarding the definition of the

---

[1] This article draws partially on the research developed within the project 'Combined and Uneven Comparisons. Rethinking the fields of African and Postcolonial literary studies within the debate on world-literature', led by Elena Brugioni from the University of Campinas (UNICAMP), grant 2020/07836-0 São Paulo Research Foundation (FAPESP). It is also the partial outcome of research conducted within the Africa Multiple Cluster of Excellence at the University of Bayreuth, funded by the Deutsche Forschungsgemeinschaft (DFG, German Research Foundation) under Germany's Excellence Strategy — EXC 2052/1 — 390713894.

[2] Kirti N. Chaudhury, *Asia before Europe: Economy and Civilization of the Indian Ocean from the Rise of Islam to 1750* (Cambridge: Cambridge University Press, 1990).

[3] Sugata Bose, *A Hundred Horizons: The Indian Ocean in an Age of Global Empire* (Cambridge, MA: Harvard University Press, 2006).

[4] Isabel Hofmeyr, 'The Black Atlantic Meets the Indian Ocean: Forging New Paradigms of Transnationalism for the Global South — Literary and Cultural Perspectives', *Social Dynamics: A Journal of African Studies*, 33.2, (2007), 3–32.

[5] Shanty Moorthy and Ashraf Jamal (eds), *Indian Ocean Studies: Cultural, Social, and Political Perspectives* (New York: Routledge, 2010).

[6] On the theoretical and conceptual revision offered by Indian Ocean studies see Meg Samuelson, 'Coastal Form: Amphibian Positions, Wider Worlds and Planetary Horizons on the African Indian Ocean Littoral', in *Comparative Literature*, 69.1 (2017), 16–24; Isabel Hofmeyr, 'The Complicating Sea: The Indian Ocean as a Method', in *Comparative Studies of South Asia, Africa and the Middle East*, 32.3 (2012), 584–90; and Elena Brugioni and Joana Passos (eds), Dossier 'Narrando o Índico', in *Diacrítica — Literatura*, 27.3 (Braga: Húmus Edições-CEHUM, 2013), pp. 7–158.

Indian Ocean as a region, an arena or rather a world-system, our premise draws on the definition of the Indian Ocean as a unit of analysis which is inevitably embedded in a singular and uneven world-system.[7]

Bearing in mind the aims of this article, two aspects emerge as particularly significant: on the one hand, the critical reflections and aesthetics related to the concept of identity, presenting conceptual developments that aim to account for situated and simultaneously anti-essentialist hybridization phenomena; on the other hand, a proposal for contextual redefinition which holds great promise for an intersection between Indian Ocean studies and the field of ecocriticism and, more broadly, of what has been defined as *environmental humanities*. In this respect, it is important to underline that the concepts of *coolitude* and *identité corail* [coral identity], within the aesthetic and critical framework proposed by Khal Torabully, offer the possibility of addressing the very concept of *environment* as a 'complex (and often conflict-ridden) web, field, or system — whatever we choose to call it — composed of the relationships between human and non-human agents or actors that define the history',[8] applicable to the Indian Ocean. Therefore, these concepts suggest the hypothesis of studying Torabully's works within the critical and theoretical perspective of what Pablo Mukherjee defines as 'eco-materialist aesthetics'.[9]

Concerning the creative potential of Indian Ocean studies in critical and conceptual terms, particular attention must be paid to identity discourses which, by dissociating from an essentialist and ethnocentric dimension, become themselves specific aesthetic and theoretical categories with strong analytical and conceptual potential for framing the concept of identity beyond a cultural and identity hybridism detached from the historical, political and material circumstances surrounding their creation. These categories would go beyond what we might call a postcolonial vulgate, that is, postcolonial as an academic label of 'celebratory' nature.[10] Rather, they could be viewed as a critical gesture

---

[7] Specifically, our premise is based on the world-system theory proposed by Fernand Braudel in the work *La Méditerranée*, vol. I: *L'Espace et l'Histoire*, and vol. II: *Les Hommes et l'Héritage* (Paris: Flammarion, 1985) and on the work of Immanuel Wallerstein, namely: Immanuel Wallerstein, *The Modern World-System: Capitalist Agriculture and the Origins of the European World-Economy in the Sixteenth Century* (New York and London: Academic Press, 1974); Immanuel Wallerstein, *The Modern World-System II: Mercantilism and the Consolidation of the European World-Economy, 1600–1750* (New York: Academic Press, 1980); Immanuel Wallerstein, *The Modern World-System III: The Second Era of Great Expansion of the Capitalist World-Economy, 1730–1840s* (San Diego, CA: Academic Press, 1989).

[8] Pablo U. Mukherjee, *Postcolonial Environments: Nature, Culture and the Contemporary Indian Novel in English* (London: Palgrave Macmillan, 2010), p. 11.

[9] As Mukherjee states: 'I share Harvey's conviction that it is impossible to understand history and geography, nature and culture, without acknowledging their mutual interpenetration. But since I have understood "environment" as being the symbiotic network of the entire human and non-human fields of existence, I have collapsed the potentially distinct terms "history" and "geography" into "eco-". Further, since I mobilize this historical-materialist concept of the environment in order to read literary cultures from a particular stage in history, I have here raised the issue of aesthetics' (p. 19). On environmental humanities see also Rob Nixon, *Slow Violence and the Environmentalism of the Poor* (Cambridge, MA: Harvard University Press, 2011).

[10] Simon During, 'Postcolonialism and Globalisation: A Dialectical Relation After All?', in

capable of questioning the intersections between territories of knowledge and power in the construction of a critical discourse whose philosophical and theoretical palimpsest is based on the conceptual constellations that unfold from the relations between the Self and the Other. It can thus be argued that theoretical concepts developed in the context of Indian Ocean Studies contribute to shifting the focus to the intersections, the relational moments that are also fundamental in many literatures in countries like Angola, Mozambique or Brazil with their entanglements in the respective literary landscapes as well as between them. Therefore, this article will present the work of a Mauritian poet, Khal Torabully, who proposes a number of concepts that could contribute to raising new research questions in Portuguese Studies as well as promoting comparative approaches among literatures written in Portuguese. A paradigmatic case can be found in Torabully's theories regarding the concepts of *coolitude* and *identité corail*.

Anchored in the theoretical discourses revolving around the so-called diasporic identities and pointing to critical constellations at the intersection between *négritude*, *créolité*, *indianité*, and *Indianocéanisme*, Khal Torabully develops the concept of *coolitude* by emphasizing space-time conditions and imaginaries that guide the human experience of the coolie (the Indian migrant in the context of indentured labour), such as the journey, the sea, the memory, the destruction, the rooting and the contact. In doing so, the author expands the coolie's conceptual and theoretical ramifications and puts forth an identitarian discourse based on the figure of the indentured worker — mostly of Indian origin — which ultimately becomes a condition: that of *coolitude*. This, in turn, is crucial to the emergence of political and aesthetic subjectivities inherent to a given spatial and temporal context, as well as to a distinct imaginary such as that of the Indian Ocean, and more pointedly to its island status as a specific geo-historical environment. Therefore, *coolitude* is based upon the experience of social marginalization, near-slave labour conditions, the loss of cultural ties, and the impossibility of returning to the country of origin as a series of conditions that set off the existence of a being in the world. Furthermore, *coolitude* is akin to the experience of diaspora and exile, of deported slaves who are exposed to the gathering of various ethnic and cultural groups in a very small space, on islands like Martinique or Mauritius. These existential experiences form the basis of a process of creolization that questions notions of hybridity grounded in the combination or fusion of two entities into something new.

At around the same time, when Torabully came up with the concept of *coolitude*, the concept of *créolité* was suggested by three Martinican writers — Jean Bernabé, Patrick Chamoiseau and Raphaël Confiant[11] — who propounded

---

Postcolonial Studies, 1.1 (1998), 31–47.
[11] Jean Bernabé, Patrick Chamoiseau and Raphaël Confiant, *Éloge de la Créolité* (Paris: Gallimard, 1989).

a more holistic view of the ongoing gatherings. These writers invited us to go beyond blackness, integrating all other ethnic and cultural groups that contributed to and participated in the coexistence, sharing and ultimately the merging of cultural practices from different origins, such as Indians, Chinese, Lebanese, Syrians, in addition to the European and African groups. The Martinican writer and philosopher Édouard Glissant proposed that *creolization* should be used instead of *créolité* in order to emphasize the continuous and endless *process* of gatherings with the intensity and quality of the impact that the multiple threads may exert on each other. In his view, the rhizome metaphor borrowed from Deleuze and Guattari played a prominent role, as it allowed him to replace the idea of a concept of identity based on rootedness and on the notion of origin (i.e., cultural, racial or ethnic) with another one, more lateral and founded on multidirectional and interconnected networks of roots, like those of a mangrove or a rhizome that evolves horizontally rather than vertically.

The similarities with the visual and political locations that represent the Middle Passage, as evidenced in the theorization proposed, for example, by Paul Gilroy about the Black Atlantic,[12] and originally developed within the scholarship on postcolonial and diaspora studies,[13] become evident here. In connection with this, it is worth highlighting the dimension of an *anti-essentialist essentialism*, which characterizes the diaspora theorized by Hall and Gilroy as a conceptual 'contact zone'[14] between the theoretical palimpsest of the Black Atlantic and *coolitude* in the Indian Ocean space-time.[15] The latter, in particular, is related to a notion of a return to Mother India but also to the concept of Kalapani ('the black sea' in Hindi language). Thus, the condition of *coolitude* would become conceptually disconnected from an identity matrix of ethnocentric nature, turning into a historical and material symbol for the dimension of cultural discourse (especially poetic discourse in the specific case of Torabully), free from a '*narrative of origins*'. At the same time, it would point to a movement and a process (the journey, the displacement, the crossing) based on a dimension of immanence (the condition of happening), rather than an essentialist/ethnocentric condition.

In this context, the possibility arises of framing the concept of *coolitude* as a historically specific and spatial ramification, or rather — and in more precise theoretical terms — a conceptual revision determined by the material and historical conditions of the Indian Ocean. In other words, a *situated concept* amenable to re-examination of the critical and political meaning of the concept of hybridity (and, by analogy, that of creolization), dismantling its merely

---

[12] Paul Gilroy, *The Black Atlantic* (London: Verso, 1993).
[13] Stuart Hall, *The Fateful Triangle: Race, Ethnicity, Nation*, ed. by Kobena Mercer (Cambridge, MA, and London: Harvard University Press, 2017).
[14] Mary Louise Pratt, *Imperial Eyes: Travel Writing and Transculturation* (London and New York: Routledge, 1992).
[15] Hofmeyr, 'The Black Atlantic Meets the Indian Ocean'.

celebratory tendency which is typically promoted by a dematerialized critical approach (i.e., postcolonial as label, disengaged with a material critical gesture). Or, to put it in other words again, a condition which is neither celebratory nor tied to the corollaries of *multicultural nomadism* and *cross-cultural hybridity* in neoliberal terms.[16] It is instead determined by historical and social contingencies established at the core of the colonial and cultural relations that materialize in the Indian Ocean regions and especially in the historical, political and cultural environment of the island(s), which represents a peculiar space-time unit within the Indian Ocean. Therefore, through the prism of Indian Ocean literatures, *coolitude* seems to favour the same critical movement underlined by Françoise Lionnet on examining the difference between *cosmopolitanism* and *creolization*.[17] The latter term, besides being a concept that focuses on the transcultural dynamics located in the so-called Third World,[18] becomes a theoretical device that does not aim to 'conceal relations of power and violence'. Instead, it regards creolization as a tactical response to a colonial situation — that is, one of 'domination and conflict' — and hence as a phenomenon permanently related to 'hierarchization, domination, subalternity, control and resistance'.[19] Theoretically, this approach draws first and foremost on Édouard Glissant's reflections but it also echoes the theses put forward by Stuart Hall[20] and Fançoise Vergès.[21] Besides this kind of conceptual revision, *coolitude* — and particularly the concept of *coral identity* (and *coral poetics*) according to the definition proposed by Torabully, which will be addressed in the second part of this article — appears to be a strategic standpoint to analyse the relationship between postcolonial critique and the environment, the so-called 'green turn' in postcolonial studies.[22] This affords an opportunity to observe how the relationship between the two fields can actually reinvigorate both approaches, overcoming limitations and blind spots that characterize environmental studies, on the one hand, and postcolonial critique on the other. On this matter,

---

[16] On the relation between neoliberalism and postcolonial critique see Sharae Deckard and Stephen Shapiro (eds), *World Literature, Neoliberalism, and the Culture of Discontent: New Comparisons in World Literature* (London: Palgrave, 2019), pp. 1–48.
[17] Françoise Lionnet and Shu-mei Shih (eds), *The Creolization of Theory* (Durham, NC, and London: Duke University Press, 2011).
[18] According to this perspective, cosmopolitanism would fall into a category spatially located in the so-called First World. For a discussion on cosmopolitanism within the Indian Ocean, see Shanti Moorthy, 'Abdulrazak Gurnah and Littoral Cosmopolitanism', in *Indian Ocean Studies*, ed. by Moorthy and Jamal, pp. 73–102.
[19] Lionnet and Shih, *The Creolization of Theory*.
[20] Stuart Hall, 'Creolization, Diaspora, and Hybridity in the Context of Globalization', in *Créolité and Creolization*, ed. by Okwui Enwezor et al. (Ostfildern-Ruit: Hatje Cantz, 2003), pp. 185–98.
[21] Françoise Vergès, 'Kiltir Kreol: Processes and Practices of Créolité and Creolization', in *Créolité and Creolization*, ed. by Okwui Enwezor et al., pp. 179–84.
[22] On this, see Graham Huggan, 'Greening Postcolonialism: Ecocritical Perspectives', in *Modern Fiction Studies*, 50.3 (2004), 701–33; Rob Nixon, 'Environmentalism and Postcolonialism', in *Postcolonial Studies and Beyond*, ed. by A. Loomba, S. Kaul and A. Burton (Durham, NC, and London: Duke University Press, 2005), pp. 233–51; and Rob Nixon, *Slow Violence and the Environmentalism of the Poor* (Cambridge, MA: Harvard University Press, 2011).

according to Pablo Mukherjee:

> [...] if eco-critical and postcolonial studies have been rendered contradictory by their absorption of the global debates about the environment, the possibility of overcoming these contradictions can also be generated from within them. By revisiting and strengthening the philosophical strains of materialism that are present in them, these theoretical fields can resolve some abiding conceptual problems and develop new ways of reading the symbiotic relationship between literary and cultural texts in relation to the environment.[23]

In his article entitled 'Coolitude between Fixity and Fluidity: Agglutination and the Poetics of the Coral',[24] Torabully presents a concise overview of his reflections in a critical dialogue with the writings of Deleuze & Guattari and Édouard Glissant. He hypothesizes the need for a critical rethinking of the concept of rhizome used by Glissant and for the replacement of that metaphor with the concept of the coral. In his view, the rhizome has a limited ability to capture the ideas of movement that are so important in Glissant's philosophy as well as in the continuous evolutions of creation processes. The explanation for his choice lies in the symbiotic nature of the coral. 'Symbiosis', a word composed of 'together' and 'life', describes a symbiotic being of a zooplankton and a phytoplankton that must find a balance to live together:

> Indeed, in the coral, a zooplankton and a phytoplankton (or alga) enter in a particular symbiotic relation. These two species have to find a balance to live together, which can be redefined and renegotiated in an unending process. There is equality in this relation, which is a prerequisite of a mature type of association and relation. [...]
>
> In this equal symbiotic negotiation, for instance, when the alga with which the coral lives quits it, it dies, both being engaged in a fifty/fifty relationship. [...] So, there is a constant and brittle negotiation of different components in the corallian structure, never the abolition of differences. It is a shared life dimension with all the will and fragility this shared space entails.[25]

Based on this specific interdependent life form, Torabully further argues that the coral is a third emerging life form that offers

> [...] a fitter support for a post hybrid scope, in which the species mediate permanently on an equality basis, to allow the emergence of a third element, from which further relations can be developed inside and outside the hybrid organism through agglutinative connectivity.[26]

In response to Glissant's philosophical reflections, Torabully introduces a new

---

[23] Mukherjee, *Postcolonial Environments*, p. 58.
[24] Khal Torabully, 'Between Fixity and Fluidity: Agglutination and the Poetics of the Coral', in *Nach der Hybridität: Zukünfte der Kulturtheorie*, ed. by Ottmar Ettea and Uwe Wirth (Berlin: Edition Tranvía, 2014), pp. 93–121.
[25] Torabully, 'Between Fixity and Fluidity', p. 110.
[26] Ibid.

concept, *coral identity*, while searching for an oceanic metaphor that would allow us to conceive of the aforementioned processes in an even more open and 'eco-critical' manner. Gesine Müller and Johanna Abel describe Torabully's approach as follows:

> The coral can be observed in its living habitat, unlike the rhizome, which exists underground. Beyond that it allows for a composite rather than just an erratic collectivity, one that grows, palimpsest-like, through layering, condensation and sedimentation, but that nevertheless retains the egalitarian aspect of its conjunctions and openness to being traversed by all currents. The coral is in its very nature a hybrid, for it is born of the symbiosis of a phytoplankton and a zooplankton. It is the perfect metaphor for diversity. It is simultaneously a root, a polyp, and a splitting; it is fluid in form, both pliant and hard, dead and alive; and beyond that, it has many colors.[27]

He suggests the metaphor of the coral, as it is a symbiotic yet balanced being which constantly changes while still remaining the coral. Torabully's reflections have evolved over the past three decades, from poems in *Cale d'étoiles* (1992) to *Coolitude* (2002) and finally to more theoretical essays that continually develop the concept of a coral poetics. By introducing the oceanic metaphor of the coral, Torabully manages to overcome the notion of hybridity and even creolization, which carry the idea of mixture, hence losing the 'original authenticity' as in the colonial context of '*métissage*', 'hybridization' — and even creolization as an ongoing process of fusion of different cultural practices and heritages. On the other hand, the coral emphasizes the unceasing negotiation between different elements, generating a new form of life that still involves the constitutive parts and the 'participants'. Since new life forms consist of the agglutination and combination of various elements, the coral can only live in a continuous process of searching for balance, which is the vital element that determines its own survival.

> Here, we can say, the process of living together never obliterates the necessity of adapting permanently within the organism itself. This complexity is absent from the rhizome which is basically a root-system in glissantian [*sic*] creolization, a vegetal. As we can see, from the two very different symbiotic elements, a third form of life emerges, the coral. This ontogenetic element of the coral offers, I believe, a fitter support for a post hybrid scope, in which the species mediate permanently on an equality basis, to allow the emergence of a third element, from which further relations can be developed inside and outside the hybrid organism through agglutinative connectivity.[28]

---

[27] Gesine Müller and Johanna Abel, 'Cultural Forms of Representation of "Coolies": Khal Torabully and his Concept of Coolitude', in *Bonded Labour: Global and Comparative Perspectives (18th–21st Century)*, ed. by Sabine Damir-Geilsdorf, Ulrike Lindner, Gesine Müller, Oliver Tappe and Michael Zeuske (Bielefeld: Transcript, 2016), p. 225.
[28] Torabully, 'Between Fixity and Fluidity', p. 110.

In addition to a 'post-hybrid' perspective, Torabully views the idea of movement as central to the poetics of relation and creation in Glissant's writings. He suggests re-examining the supposed contradiction of movement and stasis, as stated in *Introduction à une poétique du divers* (1996), where 'stasis' seems to refer to a certain idea of fixity. For Torabully, this may be a misreading, as he reminds us that the meaning of 'stasis' includes the presence and absence of movement, based on an article by the philosopher Dimitris Vardoulakis:

> Movement and immobility coexist in stasis, one being a prelude to the other and this dialectics speaks for itself. This duality of meanings generates therefore another polysemic dimension. Vardoulakis rightly asserts that: 'There is a third category of meanings in which stasis and its derivatives denote simultaneously and equally mobility and immobility, thereby undermining their opposition or mutual negation.'[29]

And further on:

> The author [Vardoulakis] offers here a marvelous example of stasis as being an expression of mobility, which also conjoins absence of movement, in the kind of sailing where the wind moves and halts, but in which stillness and motion are both coexisting and alternating, both aspects being co-substantial in what I may coin as a dynamics of 'fluixity'. Therefore, here, the word offers more than the final halt contained in Glissant's answer.[30]

It is interesting to see how Torabully develops his first idea of *coral identity* starting with his poems published in *Cale d'étoiles* (1992). These focus on the boat, the experience of being lost, of forced labour, of dying, which was the way towards the island as a new 'home' for the homeless and the people without memory, the 'coolies'. This idea of the human beings who were captured, used, reduced to a labour force, and thrown away as waste at the moment of exhaustion of this force, is highlighted by Elizabeth Deloughrey in 'heavy waters',[31] but also by Valérie Magdelaine-Andrianjafitrimo in her critical reading of some novels by Indian Ocean authors who tell the story of the abject bodies that 'populate' or even 'taint' the sea.[32] The idealizing metaphor of a 'submarine unity', of a fluid identity overcoming notions of binary identity structures so that an integrative, rhizomatic identity could come into being, is called into question:

> Certes l'océan et les espaces luminaires des plages invitent à des mélanges de temporalités, à tisser des formes de contre-narrations qui permettent aux

---

[29] Torabully, 'Between Fixity and Fluidity', p. 103.
[30] Ibid.
[31] Elizabeth Deloughrey, 'Heavy Waters: Waste and Atlantic Modernity', *PMLA*, 125.3 (2010), 703–12; on this see also Kerby Bystrom and Isabel Hofmeyr, 'Oceanic Routes: (Post-it) Notes on Hydro-Colonialism', in *Comparative Literature*, 69.1 (2017), 1–6.
[32] Valérie Magdelaine-Andrianjafitrimo, 'Is "The unity [...] submarine"? Hommes et femmes à la mer dans quelques textes des îles du Sud-Ouest de l'Océan Indien', in *Borders and Ecotones in the Indian Ocean: Cultural and Literary Perspectives*, ed. by Markus Arnold, Corinne Duboin and Judith Misrahi-Barak (Montpellier: Presses Universitaires de la Méditerranée, 2020), pp. 71–90.

fantômes d'outremer d'accéder à la visibilité et à la densité du récit. Mais ce que disent ces récits, c'est d'abord la hantise de l'altérité, la fascination terrifiée du 'débarquement' des autres, un discours sur des frontières impossibles à franchir.[33]

The ocean is a metaphor that oscillates between various attributions like movements, disconnections, allowing us to go beyond the notions of *métissage*, hybridity or the established idea of the sea as an even and stable network or as a cultural contact zone. On the other hand, the ocean is an immense concrete space — not just a surface, but a space of different depths, always in movement and populated, in other words,

> a political space of turbulent materiality, a wet ontology, not merely to endorse the perspective of a world of flows, connections, liquidities, and becomings, but also to propose a means by which the sea's material and phenomenological distinctiveness can facilitate the reimagining and re-enlivening of a world ever on the move.[34]

In Torabully's first collection of poems, *Cale d'étoiles* ('Cargo of stars', 1992), he navigates between those two poles, describing the fright of the sea, of the unknown and violent death — one that disconnects us even from traditions and origins, creating a vast 'nothingness' that obliges us either to disappear completely or to reinvent ourselves and build a new world. The ingredients are not only contributions from various travellers (in terms of languages, cultures, religions, etc.), but also violence, suffering and death. The notion of coral identity appears in the collection of poems entitled *Chair Corail* ('Coral Flesh', 1999), which captures the symbiotic being in between a living body of a zooplankton and a phytoplankton, attached to a stony or material base, turning into a being that is floating in the tides while still remaining attached.

> D'abord corail car ma mémoire mûrit aux courants
> Et folles traversées de phosphore
> Ensuite fragments pour déposer aux flancs sablonneux
> Les gemmes de sa parole
> Corail entre pierre et rhizome
> Que l'oubli a couronné d'escaliers fossiles.[35]

These lines read like the quintessence of Torabully's reflection on coral identity, which comes into being through ongoing changes and combinations of elementary particles ('phosphorus') that create precious stones and fossil buildings, a constant transformation between human and non-human forms of life that find their most prominent — and metaphorical — representative in the coral. Forgetting, memory, and the perception of the coral being, as well as of the ocean/world, are also part of this process. The different layers of the violent

---

[33] Magdelaine-Andrianjafitrimo, 'Is "The Unity [...] submarine"?', p. 86.
[34] Philip Steinberg and Kimberley Peters, 'Wet Ontologies, Fluid Spaces: Giving Depth to Volume through Oceanic Thinking', in *Environment and Planning D: Society and Space*, 33.2, (2015), 247–64.
[35] Khal Torabully, *Chair Corail: Fragments Coolies* (Petit-Bourg, Guadeloupe: Ibis Rouge, 1999), p. 81.

history of the islands and the oceans are described in the first stanza of the following excerpt from the poem titled 'Chant du bouffon à la face des fariboles' ('The jester's song in face of voidness'):

> Frange de corail, l'eau
> Relie murmures de sel
> Cette parole en gabelle
> Ce peu de joie
> Au partage du pain blanc [36]

The salt of the sea is linked to the economic interests and the exploitation of nature as well as of the workers who end up in a miserable life of hardships ('pain blanc' [white bread], 'peu de joie' [little joy]). The next stanza intensifies the description of a life full of hardships with endless working days. All hope and looking out for a better future are gone. There is no memory and therefore no present that can be transformed into a meaningful future. The narrator has to imagine his world by breaking the silence that would hide the — painful — sources of life on the island as well as the connections between springs of rivers and of seas.

> Feu rompu par la rosée pétillante
> Ô sel le miroir s'est enfin cassé
> Dans leurs yeux
>
> J'imagine la raison de l'être
> Qui cède au silence
> Cette île rendue plus proche
> Du chant de ses premiers oiseaux
> J'imagine la source
> Dont la mer est ailleurs
> Les éléments où le souffle tremble
> Ont éteint ma vision [37]

In the following stanza, the narrator recognizes that he can only speak in the name of the sea — the sea that is within him and in the cry of the people. The trespassing of all the rights is embodied in the persons who are stranded on the island. Their bodies are the words turned into 'flesh', so that the memory of the passage in the belly of the ships and in the depth of the sea is part of the inheritance passed on to the descendants. The communal experience turns into 'flesh-words', embodied words that take the coral form inside of the narrator.

> Je parle sous tutelle
> La mer à l'intérieur
> De nos cris
> Cette parole de recel
> Cette parole charnelle
> En moi coraillé [38]

---

[36] Torabully, *Chair Corail*, p. 65.
[37] Ibid.
[38] Ibid.

There are no borders between the past and the present, the narrator and the community, the sea and the memory. All entangled elements turn into a coral form engrained in the first-person narrator, which is a plural one, a coral identity.

As this short reading of a passage of *Chair Corail* shows, coral poetics were already present in the *oeuvre* of Torabully. The same is the case for the approaches of Critical Ocean Studies that plead for a multi-layered and relational understanding of the ocean as a complex biosphere as well as an integral part of a terraqueous zone in a larger perspective that can shift the meaning of 'land' and 'sea' when they are seen as a continuum. In this regard, Philip Steinberg and Kimberley Peters state the following:

> The ocean, as we have argued — through its material re-formation, mobile churning, and non-linear temporality — creates the need for new understandings of mapping and representing; living and knowing; governing and resisting. Like the ocean itself, maritime subjects and objects can move across, fold into, and emerge out of water in unrecognized and unanticipated ways.[39]

The coral metaphor implies the concepts of creolization and relationality but goes beyond them, as its semiotic layers are even more intricate, evoking the post-hybrid line of thinking and the fluxional density that strengthens the idea of a being which is positioned locally (even if temporarily) and in constant motion, within a multidirectional framework of entanglements. Having outlined the concept of the 'coral metaphor', Torabully goes even further by suggesting what he defines as '*coral poetics*':

> The coral poetics [...], beyond osmosis, miscegenation, endless movement or fusion, may well offer a concrete and metaphoric 'post hybrid' vision of human diversities coupled with the fragility of ecology interacting with migrations and economic realities.[40]

It is particularly relevant here that the idea of a multidimensional movement is deeply rooted in the material condition imposed by an uneven world-system,[41] tackling the coral poetic as a dialectical image able to register a distinctive set of relations between culture and nature, history and subjects. As we have already demonstrated in this article, Torabully developed the concept in his poems before defining it as such, twenty-five years later. It is worth underlining how the *coral identity*, and therefore the *coral poetic* proposed by the author, offer a productive counterpoint to recent theorizations in the field of ecocriticism, and particularly within the debate on eco-materialism, which seems to offer promising clues for a holistic reading of the world, as well as for a more materialistic reading of the relationship between culture and nature. As Pablo

[39] Steinberg and Peters, 'Wet Ontologies', p. 260.
[40] Torabully, 'Between Fixity and Fluidity', p. 120.
[41] Warwick Research Collective, *Combined and Uneven Development: Towards a New Theory of World-Literature* (Liverpool: Liverpool University Press, 2015).

Mukherjee states in his study on postcolonial environments:

> There has, then, been a long tradition of materialist thinking about the relationships between environment and culture. The various developments within this tradition, stretching back to the Enlightenment, give us a range of ideas about the mutual production of nature and culture, of representative tactics that exceed the normative mimetic standards, of texts that perform and embody their environments, of differentiated and specific levels of material reality that correspond to differentiated and specific stylistic and formal cultural moves. These ideas, I suggest, add a crucial dimension to the kind of interpretative framework that eco-critical and postcolonial studies (or even the product of its union, the field of 'green postcolonialism') have been trying to construct. We can begin to talk about an environmental or eco-aesthetics that offers a thoroughly worldly critical perspective. We can talk about how differently various human groups conceptualize and relate to their environments. We can map this difference on the basis of their differentiated modes of productive activities. Indeed, we can begin to talk of the economic, political and cultural production of the environment at the very moment we reject purely anthropocentric assumptions. Such an aesthetics or theory of culture I have been tentatively calling eco-materialism. [42]

In the area of francophone and anglophone literary and cultural studies on the Indian Ocean, the discussions around the concept of *coolitude* and *coral identity* have proved particularly productive, pointing to strategic possibilities for addressing the contradictions and tensions that shape identity discourses and paradigms from a critical and conceptual postcolonial perspective. Nevertheless, the intersection between the conceptual constellation proposed by Torabully and the debate on ecocriticism, and more precisely on eco-materialism, has yet to occur. Besides, it is worth noting an almost total absence of critical reception of these concepts and critical reflections in literary and cultural studies within Portuguese-speaking contexts, where the *oeuvre* of Khal Torabully (both poetic and critical) remains largely untranslated and unpublished,[43] and where the intersection between postcolonial studies and ecocriticism is not yet a common ground of critical debate.[44] This can be deemed a paradigmatic sign of the marginal and minority status of Indian Ocean studies in Portuguese, especially in the field of literary and cultural studies within a postcolonial critical perspective. Several considerations — of a historical, social, political and literary nature — stand out upon observing

---

[42] Mukherjee, *Postcolonial Environments*, p. 81.
[43] The first translation into Portuguese of Torabully's work has been published as one of the outcomes of Project NILUS in 2019, in the book edited by Ana Mafalda Leite, Elena Brugioni and Jessica Falconi, *Estudos sobre o Oceano Índico: antologia de textos teóricos* (Lisbon: Colibri, 2019).
[44] In this regard, see Jessica Falconi, 'Leituras Ecocríticas de João Paulo Borges Coelho', in *Mulemba*, 10.18 (2018), 85–96; Paulo de Medeiros, 'The Drowning of Time: Ecological Catastrophe, Dialectics, and Allegorical Realism in João Paulo Borges Coelho's *Ponta Gea* and *Água: uma novela rural*', in *A Companion to João Paulo Borges Coelho: Rewriting the (Post)colonial Remains*, ed. by Elena Brugioni, Orlando Grossegesse and Paulo de Medeiros, 2nd edn (Oxford: Peter Lang, 2020), pp. 219–48.

the literary and theoretical work developed by Torabully. These considerations hold critical and conceptual clues that seem fundamental to us to assess the critical and creative potential of the Indian Ocean in the field of literary studies, pointing to relevant conceptual ramifications in an investigation that is built upon questioning identitarian paradigms and undermining the celebratory character of the so-called postcolonial hybridisms as a generally and deeply dematerialized concept. Therefore, addressing the work of Khal Torabully appears to be a first step on the path to reorganizing critical discourses and aesthetics on identity, as well as on the relationship between culture and nature, possibly offering new critical avenues to tackle the Indian Ocean as a paradigmatic example of postcolonial environments within a singular and uneven world-system.

Combining the Uneven: Literatures of the Lusophone Indian Ocean in the Context of World-Literature — Proposal for a Theoretical Approach Applied to Mozambican Literature[1]

MARTA BANASIAK

University of Campinas (UNICAMP)/FAPESP — postdoctoral grant 2020/03902-9

The multiple theories of contemporary world literature in which we are interested appear at the end of the twentieth century and the beginning of the twenty-first century as a response to a wave of scepticism, not to say crisis, within the framework of literary studies, namely in comparative literature studies, and also to a kind of exhaustion of postcolonial studies, which seems to be valid for literary studies as well as for social sciences and cultural studies. In our view, this is due to something as obvious as the passage of time, during which, on the one hand, several new national literatures have been consolidated and, on the other, globalization has accelerated and increased the circulation of all kinds of information, trends, ideas, and thus also literatures. As a result, the space labelled 'postcolonial', which until recently seemed to represent a comfortable place for a large part of (semi-)peripheral literature, is no longer sufficient. In other words, one can easily argue that the theories of 'world(-)literature' arise somewhere at the crossroads between comparative literature and postcolonial studies. In this context, inclusivity is considered the founding principle of this new set of theories. However, in many cases, it is noticeable that inclusivity is conditioned both by the demands of the capitalist market and by a kind of neo-colonial and Eurocentric arrogance. Here we take as an example two of the most famous responses to redefining literary production on a global level: one developed at Harvard by David Damrosch and another by the French scholar Pascale Casanova.

Damrosch's approach is probably the most decentralized and comprehensive in terms of time and territory, since, for this scholar, in order to be considered part of world literature a literary work has to undergo a double process: 'first, by being read *as* literature; second, by circulating out into a broader world beyond

---

[1] This article was supported by the São Paulo Research Foundation (FAPESP), with a postdoctoral research grant no. 2020/03902-9.

its linguistic and cultural point of origin'.[2] Despite its apparent egalitarianism — for it is based solely on the idea of circulation outside its cultural context, thus having translation as one of its pillars — David Damrosch's world literature brings to the fore a significant number of works written in languages with fewer speakers, as well as authors coming from peripheral territories. This, in turn, may lead to the representativeness of these literatures being not only limited, but mainly influenced by economic and political factors directly linked to the market, that is, extraliterary factors. Damrosch's proposal perfectly exposes the workings of the market characterized by the predominance of the English and French languages. To this question, which can be considered 'economic', another one is added — the question of approval by the 'centre'. This condition is evidenced in Casanova's famous work. Her *World Republic of Letters* (2004) reveals itself to be very undemocratic, and it is precisely its intrinsic Eurocentrism that allows us to understand the rampant (neo-)colonialism prevailing in the literary market. It is quite clear that the literary republic created by Casanova has its beginning in the birth of modern European literature and expands its borders, letting in the territories which, according to the laws and rules dictated by the centre, gain relevance. In other words, Pascale Casanova's independent republic is a portrait of a franco-centric universe in which Paris plays the role of literary Mecca and whose position is defined through the capital's presumed cultural authority and economic power, translated into its position in the book market. It seems obvious that the more peripheral the origin of a literature within the world system, the more difficult and delayed is its possibility of becoming part of the World Republic of Letters, with emerging — or, if we prefer, postcolonial — literature being the last in line.

If we take into account the aforementioned language factor, we can easily guess that the task is somewhat simpler with respect to peripheral literature in English or French. In the case of African literature in Portuguese, the situation is much more complicated since even in academic works in the field of postcolonial studies developed in non-Lusophone countries, these literatures can barely find a place for themselves.

Gayatri Spivak formulates a theoretical proposal whose intention seems to be to overcome the issues linked to the capitalist system that dictates the rules of the game. In 2003, this Indian scholar published one of the best-known critiques of comparative literature studies in which she announces no more and no less than the death of the discipline, in *Death of a Discipline*. The fundamental aim of her proposal consists of the inclusion of the multiple literatures and languages, and consequently also of systems of thought and worldviews, of the Global South in the literary dialogue, as active participants in this coexistence. To this end, Gayatri Spivak proposes, on the one hand, to resurrect Area Studies as an alternative for cultural studies in the field of defining literary correspondences,

---

[2] David Damrosch, *What Is World Literature?* (Princeton, NJ: Princeton University Press, 2003), pp. 4–5.

and on the other hand to introduce the concept of planetarity. In Spivak's view, being a 'metropolitan phenomenon originating on the radical fringes of national language departments',[3] cultural studies suffers from a lack of rigour and easily falls into the stereotype of ethno-identity constructions, without exploring the specificities of the less dominant literatures (cultures), that is, ignoring the real 'epistemologies of the South'.[4] It is within this framework that Spivak suggests the alliance of comparative literature studies with Area Studies, which she considers more precise and transdisciplinary. She then proposes a mutual transformation of the two disciplines in order to find a new perspective:

> We cannot not to try to open up, from the inside, the colonialism of European national language-based Comparative Literature and the Cold War format of Area Studies and infect history and anthropology with the 'other' as the producer of knowledge. From the inside, acknowledging complicity. No accusations. No excuses. Rather learning the protocol of those disciplines, turning them around, laboriously, not only by building institutional bridges but also by persistent curricular interventions. The most difficult thing here is to resist mere appropriation by the dominant.[5]

It is on the basis of this merger between the disciplines that Spivak introduces the apparently apolitical category of planetarity, which is formulated by contrasting the planetary element with the global. The author understands the term 'global' as a virtual term, directly linked to the processes of globalization and the capitalist division of the world, which creates a precise network of domination and dependencies, whereas 'planet' is understood as something biological referring to 'an undivided "natural" space rather than a differentiated political space'.[6] Such a view that surpasses political-economic relations may indeed allow the languages (and literatures) of the southern hemisphere (for these constitute Spivak's focus) to be taken 'as active cultural media rather than as objects of cultural study by the sanctioned ignorance of the metropolitan migrant'.[7] It is clear that behind this alleged depoliticization lies hidden a very clear political and ethical statement. The author is calling for the need to abandon all remaining forms of (neo-)colonialism, imperialism and all capitalist and Eurocentric strategies, including those that guide the movements of the market and book circulation, as the only way to make the South 'not only an area to be studied but a place (or places) from which to speak'.[8] Despite a certain utopianism, Gayatri Spivak's proposal meets the need to relocate analytical methods with the goal of multiplying the contexts and places

---

[3] Gayatri Chakravorty Spivak, *Death of a Discipline* (New York: Columbia University Press, 2003), p. 8.
[4] Boaventura de Sousa Santos and Maria Paula Meneses (eds), *Epistemologias do Sul* (Coimbra: Livraria Almedina — CES, 2019).
[5] Spivak, *Death of a Discipline*, p. 11.
[6] Spivak, *Death of a Discipline*, p. 72.
[7] Spivak, *Death of a Discipline*, p. 9.
[8] Russell West-Pavlov (ed.), *The Global South and Literature* (Cambridge: Cambridge University Press, 2018), p. 7.

of enunciation, still bearing in mind the role of literary studies within the humanities. According to Emily Apter, '[a]s a text, *Death of a Discipline* attends to how a particular discipline — understood to be comparative literature but not necessarily so named — has remained as relevant as ever to rethinking the humanities'.[9]

The approach proposed by Gayatri Spivak, and especially her encouragement of a new, redesigned return to Area Studies becomes extremely valuable to us, as it points to our field of study — the Indian Ocean space — here in line with Moorthy and Jamal, who define the Indian Ocean region as 'one, among many liminal spaces of hybrid evolution, an area whose boundaries are both moveable and porous',[10] in contrast to Sugata Bose's notion of 'interregional arena'.[11]

Other theoreticians who map new possible paths to understanding the connections between various literatures depart directly from world-systems theories, taking them as the basis for their proposals. Among them, Franco Moretti is without a doubt one who deserves closer attention for he admits that his interest in Immanuel Wallerstein's work dates back to the late 1970s, and that since then he has been wondering how world-systems theory could change the way we understand literature. As he states himself, he only arrived at the answer many years later:

> I realized that world-systems analysis offered a very good way to account for the mix of 'all-inclusiveness' and chaos which had often been noticed in Modernist texts (Ulysses, The Waste Land, Cantos...), but never truly explained. In the light of world-systems analysis, these strange combinations could be recognized as an attempt to represent a world which has simultaneously become one (whence the all-inclusiveness) but full of disparities and contradictions (whence the chaos).[12]

The impact of that reflection is brought to light in the book *Opere Mondo: saggio sulla forma epica dal Faust a Cent'anni di solitudine* (1994), translated into English as *Modern Epic: The World-system from Goethe to García Márquez* (1996). In this book, Moretti analyses some masterpieces of literature from various geographical areas. These are texts that he calls 'world texts' and for which he creates the generic category of modern epic, conceived as 'an almost supercanonical form'.[13] Epic, because according to him these texts present

---

[9] Emily Apter, 'Afterlife of a Discipline', *Comparative Literature*, 57.3, Responding to the Death of a Discipline: An ACLA Forum (Summer 2005), 201–06 (p. 201).
[10] Shanti Moorthy and Ashraf Jamal, 'Introduction: New Conjunctures in Maritime Imaginaries', in *Indian Ocean Studies: Cultural, Social, and Political Perspectives*, ed. by Shanti Moorthy and Ashraf Jamal (London: Routledge, 2010), p. 4.
[11] Sugata Bose, *A Hundred Horizons: The Indian Ocean in the Age of Global Empire* (Cambridge, MA: Harvard University Press, 2009).
[12] Franco Moretti, 'World-Systems Analysis, Evolutionary Theory, Weltliteratur', *Review* (Fernand Braudel Center), 28.3 (2005), 217–28 (p. 217).
[13] Franco Moretti, *Modern Epic: The World-Systems from Goethe to García Márquez* (London and New York: Verso, 1996), p. 4.

'many structural similarities binding them to a distant past',[14] and modern 'because there are certainly quite a few discontinuities: important enough, indeed in one case — the supranational dimension of the represented space — to dictate the cognitive metaphor of the "world text" (which, in what is not just a verbal calque, recalls the "world economy" of Braudel and Wallerstein)'.[15] Bringing together his interest in modernity with the theories of Wallerstein and Braudel, Moretti indicates the eighteenth century as the initial period for the emergence of 'world texts', marking that century also as the beginning of what he calls the 'modern literary system', and which is directly linked to the international book market in the eighteenth and nineteenth centuries. Thus, *Modern Epic* opens with Goethe's *Faust* and is formed by a modest collection of eminent works from the Euro-Atlantic canon, with *One Hundred Years of Solitude* being the only representative from the southern hemisphere. Moretti's choice is thought to be based here, in some way, on a paradigm of inclusion similar to that chosen by Pascale Casanova, in which over time the centre allows for the widening of its spectrum and accepts the inclusion of literatures born outside it. Subsequently, in articles following *Modern Epic*, the Italian scholar explains that historical process by also evoking Itamar Even-Zohar's theory of literary polysystems. Reaching similar conclusions to those of the Israeli critic, Moretti explains the formation, or rather, the evolution of the modern literary system, directly linked to the book market, which is based on the circulation of books and trends in a unidirectional way — from the centre towards the semi-periphery and then to the periphery. This is, then, a constant stream in which the centre influences the (semi-)periphery, a process that is never reversed. However, this does not imply that, as it travels, the form does not change or does not assimilate into new territories. Given that the novel is always the focus of his work, Moretti points to the double construction of this literary form. According to him, the pillars of the composition of the novel are the following: the 'story', which corresponds to the 'plot', and the 'discourse', which in turn corresponds to the 'style'. Thus, while the 'plot' remains fixed and does not change throughout the 'journeys' of the novel, the style encounters all sorts of obstacles in its path. Indeed, one of the main obstacles lies in language, which varies depending on the territories. As a consequence, style is subjugated to the constant transformations that lead to the formation of the (semi-)peripheral novel:

> Italy, Brazil, Indonesia, Philippines, Japan, Bengal... The specifics obviously differ from case to case, but the formal logic is always the same: all these novels are in Gould's formula 'amalgamations of different traditions' — and all of the same kind: they mix a plot from the core, and a style from the periphery. Which means that, in the journey of novelistic models from center to the periphery of the world literary system, plots survive more

---

[14] Moretti, *Modern Epic*, p. 2.
[15] Ibid.

or less intact, whereas styles become somehow 'unglued' from them and replaced by different ones.[16]

However inclusive he aims to be, Franco Moretti cannot escape the traps of Eurocentric, or Western-centric, standard thinking either. One can easily reach conclusions to support the claim that, according to Moretti's proposal, the process of formation of the literary world-system is nothing more than the process of Westernization of (semi-)peripheral literatures, the construction of literary amalgams capable of operating in the international market. This may demonstrate how much the Western academy, even one which is avowedly left-wing, remains attached to its traditions. This posture becomes less disturbing if we focus on what we believe to be the main purpose of such a direct application of world-system theories to the literary world. In other words, literature, like the economic world, presents itself as a unique but deeply unequal system:

> One and unequal: one literature (Weltliteratur, singular as in Goethe and Marx), or perhaps, better one world literary system (of inter-related literatures); but a system which is different from what Goethe and Marx had hoped for, because it's profoundly unequal. [...] This is what unequal means: the destiny of a culture (usually a culture of periphery) is intersected and altered by another culture (from the core) that 'completely ignores it'.[17]

The essay quoted above, 'Conjectures on World Literature' (2000), served as a kind of trigger for another proposal on world literature (this time directly inspired in Immanuel Wallerstein's work), formulated by a group of researchers called Warwick Research Collective (WReC) and presented in the book titled *Combined and Uneven Development: Towards a New Theory of World-Literature* (2015). This proposal has two main keywords: *'combined and uneven development'* — a concept developed by Trotsky, which in cultural terms referred to the 'amalgamation of archaic forms with more contemporary ones' and the world-system.[18] In this case, world literature is conceived not as a way of reading or as a new, redesigned canon, but as a system that corresponds directly to the political-economic system and which is characterized by its combined and uneven nature (the latter perceived in opposition to 'different'). In other words, the collective proposes a conceptualization that is defined on the triple axis modern world-system / modernity / world-literature, in which modernity serves a double function, 'both what literature indexes or is "about" and what gives world-literature its distinguishing formal characteristics'.[19] As a fundamental characteristic it is important at this point to underline the fact that modernity, as an equally 'combined and uneven' phenomenon, is not construed

---

[16] Moretti, 'World-Systems Analysis, Evolutionary Theory, Weltliteratur', p. 225.
[17] Franco Moretti, 'Conjectures on World-Literature', *New Left Review*, 1 (Jan–Feb 2000), 54–68 (p. 56).
[18] Leon Trotsky, *History of the Russian Revolution*, trans. by Max Eastman, vol. 1 (London: Sphere Books, 1967), p. 432. Cited in WReC, p. 6.
[19] Warwick Research Collective (WReC), *Combined and Uneven Development: Towards a New Theory of World Literature* (Liverpool: Liverpool University Press, 2015), p. 15.

as a phenomenon that begins in one place (centre) and subsequently reaches the other spaces (semi-periphery and periphery), but rather as something that 'happens' throughout the system at the same time, whose effects and manifestations are uneven (unequal). Since the proposal is directly linked to the moment of imposition of materialist capitalism on the world system, the periodization chosen by the WReC researchers encompasses approximately the last two hundred years, that is, from the nineteenth century onwards, at a time when the expansion of capitalism became attached to the implementation of the colonial system(s). It is precisely this link that brings into focus the (semi-)peripheral (also European) spaces where the imposition of capitalism is confronted with the pre-existing political and cultural systems:

> To say that the forced introduction of capitalism in the historical contexts of colonialism spawned the development of new classes and groupings, and of new forms of class domination and struggle, is not, of course, to say that the social relations previously existing were simply overwritten or replaced. On the contrary, capitalism in these contexts was superimposed on the pre-existing relations, strengthening or reinforcing them in some respects or some situations, weakening or ameliorating them in others.[20]

WReC members draw attention to the complexity of the processes that inform relations on the centre–periphery axis:

> The processes of 'centralisation' (becoming 'core') and 'peripheralization' are multi-scalar, playing themselves out at multiple levels — neighbourhood, city, nation, region, macro-region — in addition to that of the world-system itself. Literature originating from (semi-) peripheral nations is very frequently produced by metropolitan writers who inhabit a 'core' relative to a 'periphery' within the (semi-)periphery itself [...].[21]

In the case of the Indian Ocean space, this situation seems particularly interesting since the implementation of the capitalist system finds here a complex and ancient intersectional mosaic of cultures and traditions that forms a deeply heterogeneous (hybrid) space, able to 'negotiate and indigenise modernity'[22] in a way which is anything but obvious.

Both Indian Ocean Studies and theories of world literature refer to the transnational dimension of literary analysis, something which is relatively recent in the field of Mozambican literature. Moreover, given the fact that the approach proposed in the present essay consists in the overlapping of two theories that have transnationalism as their foundation, it becomes necessary to explain briefly the reasons why until recently all the analytical focus was placed on national analysis. In the case of the so-called emergent and postcolonial literature, its role is easily understood considering the need to consolidate both cultural/national identity and the literary canon. This, in turn, implies

---

[20] Neil Lazarus, 'What Postcolonial Theory Doesn't Say', *Race & Class*, 53 (2011), 3–27 (p. 12).
[21] WReC, *Combined and Uneven Development*, p. 55.
[22] Moorthy and Jamal, 'Introduction: New Conjunctures in Maritime Imaginaries', p. 7.

that the need for the delimitation both of its territory and character, often in opposition to the former metropolis, was based on the firm and fixed telluric borders before the insecure opening of the seas. However, since its inception the project of constructing the so-called 'Mozambicanity' has proved a turbulent process, laden with internal tensions. Indeed, a political plan was in place for the construction of national unity, which aimed to create the 'new man' based on the Soviet model. This model promoted the erasure of the past, whether colonial or traditional, while simultaneously refusing the incorporation of any kind of identity continuities arising from either one, allowing room only for the elements which resulted from victory over colonial repression. As Jessica Falconi states,

> This way of understanding Mozambicanity translated into a radicalization of the concept of national unity, which would be threatened by any instance of difference. From this perspective, the cultural differences that always marked Mozambique were perceived as centrifugal factors and were therefore considered as potential divisions. It is clear that this interpretation of the notion of Mozambicanity translates into the institution of a border capable of delimiting and protecting what is considered national, it being identified with the struggle and the liberation movement.[23]

However, throughout its existence, literature in Mozambique has offered several discourses of the nation as an alternative to the official version, incorporating multiple places of enunciation inhabited by the most diverse subjects and actors, as well as reviving different pasts and (re)claiming the hybrid character of Mozambicanity. This situation of identitarian conflict has provided a very fertile ground for literary criticism, which has been devoted to unravelling the intricacies of the many disputed Mozambicanities. It can be easily understood that this conjuncture required a kind of centripetal movement on the part of literary criticism, which during the last decades concentrated its focus and interest on the national question, in other words, on issues directly linked to the construction of literary national identity. Although this situation is justified by the needs of time, it has caused the permanence of a kind of critical 'self-absorption', given that attempts to place Mozambican literature in the wider context have only recently begun to emerge. The approaches that interest us most at this point are those that tend to frame Mozambican literature within the Indian Ocean space and Indian Ocean Studies. However, such approaches (not only in the field of literature) are still scarce and recent. While studies pertaining to the Global South Atlantic are present and relatively well developed in the Portuguese-speaking world, including renowned scholars like Boaventura de Sousa Santos or Miguel Vale de Almeida, the Indian Ocean waves have been somewhat neglected. As Elena Brugioni states:

[23] Jessica Falconi, '"Para fazer um mar": literatura moçambicana e Oceano Índico', *Revista Diacrítica*, 27.3 (2013), 77–92 (p. 84) (all translations from this article and elsewhere are my own unless otherwise indicated).

> At the same time, critical and theoretical production regarding the Indian Ocean in the Portuguese-speaking world is rather different, still representing a very marginal framework, even in the fields of maritime study, slave trade history and social history in general.[24]

It is precisely scholars like Elena Brugioni or Jessica Falconi who first ventured into mapping this new critical approach to Mozambican literature. Noting the reciprocity between Indian Ocean Studies and this national literature, Jessica Falconi underlines that

> In the particular case of the topics of this reflection — Mozambican literature and the Indian Ocean — a trend of mutual inclusion paves the way for fruitful articulations, given on the one hand the insistence on the inclusion of African coasts and archipelagos in the Indian Ocean arena, and on the other hand the more recent opening towards an 'Indian' outlook on Mozambican literature.[25]

Indian Ocean Studies, as the first step towards a new outlook on Mozambican literature, is gaining ground as a more logical and natural choice, not only due to the geographical position of the country, but mainly due to the strong presence of the Indian Ocean in the literary production of Mozambique.

This area of study aims to revisit the national literary canon from a broader theoretical and critical viewpoint, which allows for multiple reinterpretations of canonical works, as well as interpretations of more recent works. It further aims to examine the centrifugal declensions of Mozambican literature vis-à-vis the national question, in search of the most comprehensive belonging.

Previously, we referred to the fact that Mozambican literature has incorporated multiple identitarian elements that form an alternative to the official version promoted by the state, which in turn has led literary criticism to place its focus on the attempt to define the concept of Mozambicanity. However, a large part of those elements is directly linked to the influence of the Indian Ocean, to the relationship of the country and its inhabitants with the sea, or even to the representation of the country's ethnic composition.

Jessica Falconi notes that

> islands and port cities are privileged places from which to think of the ocean as a network, because they represent the idea of intersection, in the dual meaning of hybridization and crossing. From this perspective, a first point of articulation between Mozambican literature and the Indian Ocean, useful to highlight convergences and specificities, is given by the representation of the Island of Mozambique.[26]

The almost mythical place of the Portuguese discoveries, peopled by historical

---

[24] Elena Brugioni, 'Behind So Many Names the Sea: Mozambique and the Indian Ocean', in *Fluid Networks and Hegemonic Powers in the Western Indian Ocean*, ed. by Iain Walker, Manuel João Ramos and Preben Kaarshom, 1st edn, vol. 1, (Lisbon: Centro de Estudos Internacionais do Instituto Universitário de Lisboa, 2017), pp. 65–80 (pp. 67–68).
[25] Falconi, '"Para fazer um mar"', p. 79.
[26] Falconi, '"Para fazer um mar"', p. 79.

figures of the empire such as Vasco da Gama and Luiz Vaz de Camões, serves concurrently as a starting point to understanding the possible developments and multiple openings of Mozambicanity. The first capital of the Province of Mozambique, a place which, on the one hand, is marked by the horrors of the slave trade, and, on the other, is regarded as a Lusotropicalist paradise, has represented since the colonial era a sacred territory in Mozambican literature. Taking as reference the emblematic work of the poets Rui Knopfli, Luís Carlos Patraquim and Eduardo White, Falconi considers the Island of Mozambique (and the Indian Ocean space) as a synecdoche of the nation,

> which assumes the relational dimension, transnationality and 'Indicity' as constitutive elements of a non-essentialist 'Mozambicanity', less founded on the integration of distinct identity elements than on the constant mobility of relations between these elements.[27]

Although the Island of Mozambique is mainly visited by poets, their prose representations can easily be subsumed into the interpretative proposal mentioned above. We are referring to works such as the short story 'O pano encantado' [The Enchanted Cloth] (2005) by João Paulo Borges Coelho, which addresses the topic of the Islamic brotherhoods in the north of the country, previously undiscussed in Mozambican literature, or the recent novel by the young author Sérgio Raimundo, *A Ilha dos Mulatos* [The Island of Mulattos] (2020). The latter appears as a bold critical deconstruction of this paradigmatic place. In his novel, Raimundo evokes the idea of the Island as the 'lupanar of history',[28] by addressing various levels of the decadence in the life of an apparently 'normal' family. In doing so, he assigns nearly dystopian characteristics to the Island of Mozambique, building a world where nobody wants to live anymore. 'Disgusting is the house of slaves that every day allows itself to be devoured by the waters. [...] Disgusting is the Island that one day will disappear, but that every day deceives us with its passing presence',[29] writes the young author, comparing the Island of Mozambique to a kind of abject Mozambicanity, 'abject' being understood according to Julia Kristeva's proposal, as follows:

> If it be true that abject simultaneously beseeches and pulverizes the subject, one can understand that it is experienced at the peak of its strength when that subject, weary of fruitless attempts to identify with something on the outside, finds the impossible within; when it finds that the impossible constitutes its very being, that is no other than abject.
> The abjection of self would be the culminating form of that experience of the subject to which it is revealed that all its objects are based merely on the inaugural loss that laid the foundations of its own being.[30]

[27] Falconi, '"Para fazer um mar"', p. 87.
[28] Nelson Saúte and António Sopa, *A Ilha de Moçambique pela voz dos poetas* (Lisbon: Edições 70, 1999), p. 53. A *lupanar*, from the Latin *lupa* (meaning 'prostitute'), is a synonym for brothel.
[29] Sérgio Simão Raimundo, *A Ilha dos Mulatos* (Lisbon: INCM, 2020), p. 104.
[30] Julia Kristeva, *Powers of Horror: An Essay on Abjection* (New York: Columbia University Press, 1982), p. 5.

It is thus our understanding that the Island in the novel is portrayed in terms of refusal, expulsion, and hence abjection, of its constitutive and permanent discourses and paradigms, while at the same time acknowledging the impossibility to dissociating itself from them. Despite this, the book announces the disappearance of the Island, since 'my family evaporated you all and the Island was dissolved by the water'.[31] Therefore, returning to this space symbolizes a paradox, an inability to change or to start afresh, unless that rebirth is brought about by the waters of the Indian Ocean.

As the space constraints in the current essay do not allow for a more in-depth analysis of the literary texts, this brief outline dedicated to Mozambique Island serves to prove the importance of the island's space and maritime imaginary in the Mozambican discursive and cultural sphere. However, the ways of conceiving the Indian Ocean in Mozambican literature are obviously not limited only to the geographical and discursive space of the Island of Mozambique. In fact, they have an important role to play in the work of authors such as João Paulo Borges Coelho and Mia Couto, two of the most prominent Mozambican novelists.

In the case of Mia Couto, the most famous novelist in Mozambican literature, the presence of the Indian Ocean permeates several of his novels and often constitutes the complicating element of the so-called Mozambicanity, where the sea represents the founding space of cultural and identity diversity, as well as the refuge and liberating space. The 1996 novel *A Varanda do Frangipani* [*Under the Frangipani*] begins with a quotation by Eduardo Lourenço, who sees Mozambique as 'an immense balcony over the Indian Ocean'. This metaphor is the key to the novel, most of which takes place in an old fortress facing the sea, transformed into a care home for the elderly. By using Lourenço's metaphorical image, Mia Couto creates a national metonymy, through the image of that fortress inhabited by multiple characters, some who arrived there by land and others from the other side of the ocean. Or rather, he creates a small, closed microcosm, a complex and hybrid world that is now under threat, representing an unused past, isolated and guarded by the sea. As one of the characters says: 'All I have left is this little space where I am shaded by the sea. My nation is a balcony.'[32] A similar turn towards the Indian Ocean also takes place in the author's previous and most popular novel, *Terra Sonâmbula* [*Sleepwalking Land*] (1992), which tells us about the country devastated by the sixteen-year-long war. In this country, the relationship between sea and land translates into a relationship between cruel reality and turbulent dream, where a war-torn land seems to float aimlessly like a lost boat. In the words of Meg Samuelson, '[t]he land has journeyed to the sea of stories on which it is set adrift, while narratives crafted in these waters disintegrate into the grains of sand that comprise it.'[33]

---

[31] Raimundo, *A Ilha dos Mulatos*, p. 139.
[32] Mia Couto, *A Varanda do Frangipani* (Lisbon: Caminho, 2007), p. 23.
[33] Meg Samuelson, 'Coastal Form: Amphibian Positions, Wider Worlds and Planetary Horizons on the African Indian Ocean Littoral', *Comparative Literature*, 69.1 (2017), 16–24 (p. 20).

Furthermore, in this novel the Indian Ocean emerges as an inexhaustible source of the country's multiplicity and complexity in terms of identity:

> And he passed on a thought to me: we, those of the coast, were inhabitants not of a continent, but of an ocean. Surendra and I shared the same homeland: the Indian Ocean.
> And it was as if in that immense sea the threads of history were unwinding, ancient balls of thread where our bloods had mingled. This is the reason why we lingered in the adoration of the sea: there lay our common ancestors, floating boundlessly.[34]

However, one easily perceives that the maritime element in those narratives, as opposed to the telluric, is characterized by a kind of centrifugal force that pulls towards the open, the immeasurable, far exceeding the limitations of the so-called 'national' or 'local'. This becomes even more visible in the novel *O Outro Pé da Sereia* [*The Mermaid's Other Foot*] (2006), which contains a multiplicity of gazes, presenting a multidirectional and transnational structure. Within this framework, the Indian Ocean is viewed as a foundational space, not only of Mozambicanity but of the many other identities. It is from the Indian Ocean and through the Indian Ocean that an intercontinental genetic relationship is formed, whereby the oceanic crossing takes on demiurgic contours. Indeed, it is during the crossing of the Indian Ocean that the young Catholic priest, Antunes, begins to sever his link with faith, which will later lead him to a very different spiritual path, already in Africa — an episode which undoubtedly symbolizes the deconstruction of the European identity. It is also during this crossing that an Indian woman, Dia Kumari, and an African man, Nimi Nsundi, conceive a son who, after crossing the other ocean, could be the ancestor of the African-American historian Benjamin Southman. Thus, with the Indian Ocean as a kind of canvas, a picture of interdependence is drawn between historical events and phenomena around the world, portraying Mozambique as an equal participant in these events and, at the same time, as a space which is subject to the consequences of (inter)national occurrences.

As previously noted, another author whose work draws on 'oceanic fecundity' is João Paulo Borges Coelho. Within his already extensive prose, the collection of ten short stories titled *Índicos Indícios* (2005) stands out in this regard. It is divided into two volumes, *Setentrião* and *Meridião*, 'following a criterion that is merely geographic',[35] and maps the Mozambican coast and its islands from north to south. Although each of the tales could easily fit within the scope of this essay, it will only be possible to mention one, namely 'Casas de Ferro' [Iron Houses]. This short story mixes fiction with reality, as is typical in Borges Coelho's writing. It focuses on the eviction process of the residents of the 'skeleton' of the Grande Hotel da Beira and the transition to their 'new' address. The Grande Hotel, built in the colonial era in the 1950s and considered

---

[34] Mia Couto, *Terra Sonâmbula* (Lisbon: Leya, 2010), p. 25.
[35] João Paulo Borges Coelho, *Índicos Indícios*, I: *Setentrião* (Lisbon: Caminho, 2005), p. 9.

the largest hotel in Africa, had a few glorious years. Abandoned and neglected, at the time of independence it became the space of free housing, sheltering up to 3,100 families, without access to water or electricity. In the story, the residents of the Hotel are being removed from their habitat by the 'Authorities' who are driven by the

> old obligation to promote Development, keeping them away from the bay that the tourists of the future will enjoy, from the air they were going to breathe — standing on the balconies that will be built after the hammer concludes the noisy activity — that scenario of rubbish and tragedy.[36]

Left to their fate, the population of the Hotel finds refuge in the carcasses of the old boats stranded by the sea. These boats are, as Giulia Spinuzza remarks, 'traces of the past and testify, along with the hotel, to a prolific time in which large vessels arrived and left full of goods and raw materials'.[37] However, due to maritime movements, they have become disconnected from the land, turning into islands. Spinuzza continues:

> In 'Iron Houses', JPBC invents a possible future for its inhabitants. The story, centred on the displacement of part of the community from the hotel to the boats stranded on the beach, can also be read as a metaphorical journey of the country. The boats, as new islands outside the territory of the nation, point to an 'other' reality that moves away from the connection to the land and into the space of the Indian Ocean. The People of the stranded ships, shipwrecked in their own country, also open up to the horizon of the Indian Ocean. Then, the writing reinvents and rewrites the nation according to new paradigms, and fiction blends with reality, memory and history.[38]

In the essay where she delimits the category of coastal literature, in which she also includes Couto's *oeuvre* — and that, in our opinion, should also encompass much of the work of Borges Coelho and other authors mentioned — Meg Samuelson notes that

> A variant on the inside-outside binary is that of universalism versus nationalism. In external constructions, Africa has long been cast as a land set apart from the currents of world history. Although 'African modes of self-writing,' as Achille Mbembe shows, have emerged in response to the world-destroying practices of slavery and colonialism that were justified through this denial of its worldliness, they also reiterate the colonial episteme by equating 'identity with race and geography,' rejecting 'a politics of the universal,' and seeking to restore subjectivity and sovereignty through assertions of 'cultural uniqueness' and 'autochthony'. [...] In the Indian Ocean, these apparently opposed terms enfold. Sugata Bose finds

---

[36] João Paulo Borges Coelho, 'Casas de Ferro', in *Índicos Indícios*, I: *Setentrião* (Lisbon: Caminho, 2005), p. 70.

[37] Giulia Spinuzza, 'Olhares cruzados sobre o Grande Hotel da Beira: "Hóspedes da noite", de Licínio de Azevedo, e "Casas de Ferro", de João Paulo Borges Coelho', *Revista Cerrados*, 25.41 (2016), 276–87 (p. 284).

[38] Spinuzza, 'Olhares cruzados', p. 285.

that even in the age of global imperialism, 'nationalism and universalism' were therein 'bound in a strong symbiotic embrace' rather than arranged into 'an adversarial relationship' (31). Unlike the formations of 'Africa' and the 'Black Atlantic,' a critical understanding of the Indian Ocean 'complicates binaries, moving us away from the simplicities of the resistant local and the dominating global' (Hofmeyr, 'Universalizing', 722).[39]

In fact, the short story 'Casas de Ferro' is the perfect example of combining the two proposed theoretical paths, Indian Ocean Studies and World-Literature, as it provides an apt representation of the effects of combined and uneven development. The short story depicts a kind of game where failed modernization, embedded in the attempts of centralization, cyclically find the peripheral answer, unexpected, and rather creative. Let us consider the first great capitalist project, the construction of the largest hotel in Africa, which meets its ending as a peripheral reinvention, becoming not only the house but the entire operational mode of a community. Subsequently, that community, subject to the second wave of marginalization by the hotel renovation project, repurposes other capitalist debris — the stranded boats. Paradoxically, this seeming exclusion could easily be interpreted as an opening if we focus on the maritime element, as claimed by Spinuzza in the above-quoted passage, which announces the endless reinvention skills.

As we have intended to show, Mozambican literature has long portrayed the topics linked to the incorporation of the Indian Ocean heritage and to the placement of the plot in the coastal zone (the importance of the sea, or representations of the cultural and ethnic elements coming from the Indian zone) as being integral to Mozambican identity. At the same time, these works clearly reflect the political and social turbulences that, through the maritime metaphorical field, project their interpretation onto wider contexts.

Concerning the relations between the different literatures of the Indian Ocean, Portuguese-speaking and others, Nazir Can regrets the almost non-existent 'representation, in national literatures, of the social and historical realities of the other countries or departments that form part of the region. One can even state, [he says,] with a certain degree of certainty, that Indian Ocean productions suffer from a common symptom, a kind of introverted insularity, for they represent, with rare exceptions, only their own internal spaces.'[40] However, it is important to ask ourselves if this is necessarily a problem, in other words, if it is vital to have this reciprocal representation of the various segments of the Indian Ocean in the respective literatures. Is this not an easily exhaustible source?

Placing the Indian Ocean literatures, and in this particular case Mozambican literature, within the analytical paradigm proposed by the WReC allows us to

---

[39] Samuelson, 'Coastal Form', p. 18.
[40] Nazir Ahmed Can, 'Índico em Moçambique: notas sobre o outro', *Revista Diacrítica*, 27.3 (2013), 93–120 (p. 95).

reposition our research. We can drive away the concern regarding the almost non-existence of reciprocal representation among the various literatures that compose the Indian Ocean system and focus precisely on finding possible similarities in the approaches, the topics and — why not? — the predominant literary forms. In other words, rather than trying to find a direct exchange or dialogue, this approach can work as a kind of photographic lens, which enables us to adapt our perspective by zooming in or out: Farther away — global-capitalist, (semi-)peripheral, Indian Ocean, 'Lusophone' Indian Ocean, with the national level preventing these categories from becoming contradictory and instead making them work as layers of a whole.

Literature in Transit between Goa and Mozambique: Campos Oliveira as a Pioneering Figure

ANA MAFALDA LEITE and JOANA PASSOS

University of Lisbon/CEsA / University of the Minho

Introduction

Although our research is centred on the figure of José da Silva Campos Oliveira (1847–1911), our study also offers a background reflection on the circulation of literary trends from Goa and Mozambique at the transition from the nineteenth to the twentieth century. In theoretical terms, our research is framed by the academic debate on Indian Ocean Studies, and we aim to contribute to the history of cultural dynamics in the region. We will rely on a comparative approach, relating literary life in Goa to the first initiative to start a literary magazine in Mozambique. In this way, we believe we are answering the challenge issued by thinkers such as Carpanin Marimoutou and Françoise Vergès,[1] or Isobel Hofmeyr,[2] who argue for the need to study cultural dynamics between different nations or communities from the Indian Ocean in order to compile and disseminate a view of local regional history on its own terms, outside the Eurocentric perspectives which have been dominant in the established knowledge that has circulated internationally.

As we recovered fragmentary information on Campos Oliveira's life and work, we realized he provided an interesting case study of the role played by local citizens in the development of cultural initiatives, independently of state-sponsored activities. Furthermore, as he lived in Goa and in Mozambique, his journey also reflects the logical connection between sea routes which were used to move people and goods and the possibility of cultural exchange and transfer across the Indian Ocean. In other words, we believe the flow of people along migratory sea routes has had a cultural impact as a powerful means of disseminating cultural influences from coast to coast, beyond the circumscribed spaces that nurtured the development of national literatures.

Another point worth mentioning is that our study of Campos Oliveira features a contribution from the eastern coast of Africa (and in the Portuguese

---

[1] Françoise Vergès and Carpanin Marimoutou, 'Moorings: Indian Ocean Creolizations', in *Portal: Journal of Multidisciplinary International Studies*, 9.1 (2012), 1–39.
[2] Isobel Hofmeyr, 'Universalizing the Indian Ocean', *PMLA*, 125 (2021), 721–29.

language) to the sphere of Indian Ocean Studies. This is innovative research, which balances the attention devoted to islands, on the one hand, and to the trade and migration routes between India and Southeast Asia, on the other, considering works by such established authors as Marimoutou, Vergès, Lionnet and Hofmeyr. The Arab port cities of the eastern coast of Africa seem to have been neglected, as were the bonds between Goa and Mozambique from the sixteenth century onwards. Apparently researchers have neglected alternative dynamics between the two latter territories, which went far beyond their shared colonial affiliation to the Portuguese Crown as there was room for private initiative to emigrate, or to move back and forth across extended family connections, as both Goans and Hindu traders (especially from Gujarat) did.

Finally, studying the life and work of Campos Oliveira is to contribute insightful information to the literary history of Mozambique, beyond routine references to his name or the sheer oblivion to which he has been consigned. By rediscovering Campos Oliveira, we are antedating the beginning of printed, modern literature in Mozambique by Rui de Noronha (1909–1943), who is often considered the first poet of Mozambique, and whose only book was published in 1943.

It is true that the works by Campos Oliveira are scattered across different periodical publications and that he was not a very prolific writer. Maybe these two facts can explain why he has eluded the attention of most scholars. However, as we will prove, he was an important figure in his own time. As contemporary literary studies are increasingly receptive to the authors of the periodical press, the likes of Campos Oliveira are finding their way towards critical acknowledgment. This inclusive view of literary studies makes all the more sense if one considers that the periodical press and leisure magazines compensated for the likely absence of a library, and softened the remoteness from a more cosmopolitan, urban culture one might have yearned for. It was because of the press that the public had access to texts and ideas, as well as the news, and newspapers also provided the only possible access to publishing opportunities for many local writers in the mid-nineteenth century.

Having claimed that Campos Oliveira has eluded most critics, it is also true that we are not the first to approach his work. A study in some depth was carried out by Manuel Ferreira, who published the essay *O Mancebo e Trovador Campos Oliveira*, in 1985. We have relied on Ferreira's work for biographical information and for references of works published by Campos Oliveira. Our knowledge was then expanded by another, more thorough study, by António Sopa, a Mozambican historian, who published his article on Campos Oliveira in 1988, in issue number 4 of the Mozambican journal *Arquivo* (actually, Ferreira received several indications from Sopa, even if the latter's work was published afterwards). In the development of our own work, we will quote Sopa's discoveries extensively. Ana Mafalda Leite also mentions Campos Oliveira in her works on the literary history of Mozambique,[3] as do M. Agostinho Matias Goenha,[4] and A. Hohlfeldt & F. Grabauska.[5]

The Author, his Time and his Legacy

José Pedro da Silva Campos Oliveira was born in 1847, on the Ilha de Moçambique, the first capital city of the country. He would become the first Mozambican poet and journalist, publishing his works in several periodical publications. According to Alexandre Lobato,[6] by the mid-nineteenth century the town's elite used to meet at literary evenings which provided local poets with the opportunity to speak aloud their Romantic lines.[7] There was a theatre company as well, sponsored by the government, which had a theatre built in 1898. Among the plays performed there, documents mention a play by the famous Almeida Garrett, entitled *D. Filipa de Vilhena*. There were literary societies, such as the *Grémio Literário*, and some of these societies had small libraries on their premises.

The small, educated circles in the main towns — not only on the Ilha but also in Quelimane or Tete — would be the public for the first literary creations in the territory, and as such they encouraged the advent of a local literature. The members of these literary circles were the so-called 'Filhos da Terra' (educated Africans or Africans of Portuguese descent who had had access to a westernized education), the military corps stationed in Mozambique, and colonial civil servants.

Printing facilities were introduced in 1854, and the first local newspapers went into operation. It is through this colonial press that a writing culture (in Portuguese) took root in the territory, allowing room for the publication of tentative literary creations by local writers, while, at the same time, disseminating texts from abroad among Mozambican publics. In May 1854, the first periodical publication was released; called *Boletim do Governo da*

---

[3] Ana Mafalda Leite, 'Tópicos para uma história da literatura moçambicana', in *Moçambique das palavras escritas*, ed. by Margarida Calafate Ribeiro and Maria Paula Meneses (Porto: Edições Afrontamento, 2008), pp. 47–76.
[4] M. Agostinho Matias Goenha, *Textes des quatre conférences données à l'Université PARIS 8, June 2010* <https://www.bu.univ-paris8.fr/web/actualites/documents_actu/ConferencesAgostinhoGoenha.pdf> [accessed January 2021].
[5] Antonio Hohlfeldt and Fernanda Grabauska, 'Pioneiros da imprensa em Moçambique: João Albasini e seu irmão', *Sociedade Brasileira de Pesquisa em Jornalismo*, 6.1 (2010), 195–214.
[6] Alexandre Lobato, *Sobre 'Cultura Moçambicana': reposição de um problema e resposta a um crítico* (Lisbon: n.pub., 1952), p. 19.
[7] We are referring to the influence of late Portuguese Romanticism, also known as third-wave Romanticism or 'Ultrarromantismo'. It is defined by the cult of motives, themes and settings inherited from Romanticism but exacerbated to the extreme, expressing a fascination for melancholia, madness, death, and a destructive boredom that disconnects the subject from the world around him/her. The favourite settings are inspired by the Middle Ages and dark Gothic. It was still popular among poets in Goa and Mozambique as late as the 1890s. In Portuguese literature, the model writers for this trend were Almeida Garrett (1799–1854) and Alexandre Herculano (1810–1877).

Província de Moçambique, it would last, under different names, until 1975. It included pieces of news and a few creative pieces — poems, chronicles and short prose pieces — side by side with more formal, official texts, which were the real reason that justified the investment in printing facilities. Soon, other periodical publications followed the official press.[8]

In the second half of the nineteenth century, one of the main names in literary circles on Mozambique Island was José Pedro da Silva Campos Oliveira (1847–1911),[9] who, as mentioned above, is considered the first locally born poet writing in Portuguese in that territory. The author was born in Cabaceira (a small town on a peninsula facing Mozambique Island), of Goan descent on his father's side.[10] His parents were local landowners, and their lives were comfortable enough to send young Campos Oliveira to Goa, India, to attend primary school and to pursue further studies. He finished high school at the Liceu Nacional de Nova Goa (in Panaji, Goa), with a major in Latin and French. He lived in Goa until 1867, when he returned to Mozambique Island. Once settled back in his hometown, he held several positions as a civil servant, including Head of the Post Office and Notary for the Port Authority.[11]

He started his literary and journalistic activity while he was still living in India, collaborating with diverse periodicals such as the newspaper *O Ultramar* (1859–1941) and the literary magazine *Illustração Goana* (1864–66), as well as the (yearly) leisure publications *Almanach Literário* (1865) and *Almanach de Lembranças Luso-Indiano* (1864, 1865, 1866). As editor, he was responsible for the *Almanach Popular* for the year of 1865, a role he would keep in later editions, even after moving to Mozambique.

In Mozambique, Campos Oliveira collaborated with several newspapers, for example, *O Progresso* (published first in a single edition, 9 April 1868, and then 1877–81), *O Jornal de Moçambique* (1873–75), *Noticiário de Moçambique* (1872) and *África Oriental* (1872). Beyond his repeated collaboration with the press, he owned and edited the first literary magazine in Mozambique, the *Revista Africana*, published between 1881 and 1885. In this period (from 1868 onwards) he also published some of his poems in leisure periodicals that circulated in Portugal.[12]

---

[8] Ilídio Rocha, *Catálogo dos periódicos e principais seriados de Moçambique da introdução da tipografia à independência, 1854–1975* (Lisbon: Edições 70, 1985).
[9] Manuel Ferreira, *O Mancebo e Trovador Campos Oliveira* (Lisbon: INCM, 1985).
[10] Manuel Ferreira states the following: 'já os seus avós residiam na Ilha de Moçambique como ele próprio refere numa das suas crónicas na *Revista Africana* [...]' [His grandparents already lived on Mozambique Island, as he himself declares in one of his chronicles in the *Revista Africana*]. See Manuel Ferreira, *O Mancebo e Trovador Campos de Oliveira*, p. 127. In this essay, Ferreira compiles 31 poems by Campos de Oliveira.
[11] A study by historian António Sopa on the biography of the poet and the epoch he lived in is the source for the majority of this information. See António Sopa, 'Campos Oliveira: jornalista e escritor moçambicano (1854–1911)', *Arquivo: Boletim do Arquivo Histórico de Moçambique*, 4 (1988), 105–44.
[12] Notably *Almanach de Lembranças Luso-Brasileiro*, *Novo Almanach de Lembranças Luso-Brasileiro*, *Artes e Letras*.

Apparently, there were six issues of *Revista Africana* (initially conceived as a monthly periodical). However, we only found incomplete copies from three issues at the National Library of Portugal, starting with the initial issue from March 1881 ('1º ANNO, nº 1'). This issue contains a note stating that the publication had been suspended until 1885, and indeed the other two numbers available are from 1885 (1 October, issue 1, and 1 November, issue 2). Even though these issues are incomplete, they testify to the fact that, in his time, Campos Oliveira helped to enliven literary activity in the first capital of Mozambique and that he was determined enough to take the initiative himself. As for his motives, the author clearly states his purpose in the introduction to the first issue of the magazine. The creation of a literary magazine is intended to cultivate interest in reading and writing among local young people, bringing them cultural articles, local news, short stories and other literary creations. In fact, the heading of issue 1 of *Revista Africana* states this very aim in its own title: '*Revista Africana* — Periódico Mensal de Instrucção e Recreio — Director e Proprietário J. P. da Silva Campos Oliveira' [monthly periodical for education and leisure — director and owner J. P. da Silva Campos Oliveira] ('1º ANNO, Março de 1881'). By contrast, issue 1 from 1885 only says '*Revista Africana* — Publicação Mensal — Director J. P. da Silva Campos de Oliveira'. Curiously, below this changed heading, the introduction from 1881 is reprinted, probably because the aims of the literary magazine remained the same (we will return to this subject below).

According to the research developed by Manuel Ferreira, Campos Oliveira also saw to the publication (as a supplement to the *Novo Almanach de Lembranças Luso-Brasileiro* of 1888)[13] of a few verses that he claimed were unpublished works by the poet Thomaz António Gonzaga ('Uns versos inéditos de Gonzaga'), which he had found as an unsigned manuscript. Gonzaga was a Portuguese/Brazilian poet (1744–1810), who died in Mozambique, seventy years before the publication of Campos Oliveira's supplement. We do not have information to assess the grounds for this claim, but it is worth pointing out that Campos Oliveira acknowledged the importance of preserving for posterity such works by publishing them, a gesture that speaks to his dynamic role as a scholar.

Ten years later, in 1891, Campos Oliveira was invited to write a preface to the first collection of poetry ever published on the Island of Mozambique. It was called *Sons Orientais* [Eastern Sounds], and its author, Artur Serrano, explains

---

[13] Campos de Oliveira wrote the following: 'N'um exemplar das Lyras do desventurado poeta Thomaz António Gonzaga, que falleceu n'esta cidade de Moçambique, em 1809 [1810], encontrei, em letra manuscripta, uns versos que embora não trouxessem por baixo o nome do author, facilmente mostram, pelo estylo e pelo assumpto, serem da lavra do distincto poeta brazileiro. [...] Eis os versos: 'A Moçambique, aqui, vim deportado, / Descoberta a cabeça ao sol ardente; / Trouxe por irrisão duro castigo. / Ante a africana, pia, boa gente. / Graças, Alcino amigo / Graças à nossa estrella! // Não esmolei, aqui não se mendiga; / Os africanos peitos caridosos / Antes que a mão o infeliz lhe estenda / A socorrel-o correm pressurosos. / Graças, Alcino amigo / Graças à nossa estrella!".' Cf. Ferreira, *O Mancebo e Trovador Campos de Oliveira*, p. 41, n. 1.

that he had asked the only poet they had on the island ('o único poeta que possuímos') to grant him the honour of writing a preface to his book.[14] This episode reveals public acknowledgment at local level and suggests Campos Oliveira was able to encourage other authors to publish their first attempts at literary writing in Mozambique.

At the time, the models for literary writing in the Mozambican capital (and other Portuguese-speaking towns on the eastern coast of Africa) were Portuguese and French authors. One can deduce this from the texts, chronicles and poems published by Campos Oliveira, including the preface mentioned above, as well as from the translated notes and quotes in *Revista Africana*. Some of his main references among French authors are Alexandre Dumas, Victor Hugo and Alphonse de Lamartine, but equally recurrent are the Portuguese writers Camilo Castelo Branco, Bernardim Ribeiro, Teófilo Braga and Gomes Leal, to mention but a few of his favourite references.

Among the set of poems by Campos Oliveira compiled by Manuel Ferreira in his book *O Mancebo e Trovador Campos Oliveira* (1985), we selected as an example of his writing the poem 'O Pescador de Moçambique' [The Fisherman of Mozambique] because in its lines the poet defines himself in relation to the sea, using his activity and his life on the water to express affiliation to the land. Furthermore, bearing in mind the importance of Mozambique Island and of the Indian Ocean as a literary *locus* in the literature of Mozambique, this poem is all the more relevant because it relates to what would become a twentieth-century literary motif throughout the works by Nelson Saúte and António Sopa (*A Ilha de Moçambique*, 1992), Luís Carlos Patraquim (*Monção*, 1981; *Inadiável Viagem*, 1985) and Eduardo White (*Amar sobre o Índico*, 1987). In addition, even if it is a fact that, among all the poems by Campos Oliveira, this is possibly the single one that expresses a sense of belonging to water coordinates rather than land ones, it is also the one that most elegantly fits the issues under discussion in this article. Besides, it represents a typical activity of the coastal regions of Mozambique, associating a community to its life on the sea. Lastly, this is an interesting poem for its racial comment, as it reclaims a black skin as one's identity,[15] an indicator of lineage that overlaps sea, race, community and

---

[14] According to the manuscript provided by Mozambican historian António Sopa, Artur Mateus Serrano was a civil servant by the end of the nineteenth century. He worked under José de Almeida at the so-called 'resident council', which was sent to Gungunhana's court. His book, *Sons Orientais* [Eastern Sounds] was published on the Island of Mozambique and is considered the first collection of poetry published in Mozambique. Around the 1880s, the position of 'residente' was created with the aim of providing counselling to the emperor on the policies to be followed. Later on, Artur Mateus Serrano turned to private initiative, having edited a newspaper in Lourenço Marques under the title *A Situação*. The above quote is from the introduction to his *Sons Orientais* (Lourenço Marques: Imprensa Nacional, 1891).

[15] Although the poetic voice claims a black identity for the fishermen of Mozambique, it may be relevant to point out that there is also an important community of Goan fishermen in Mozambique. On this topic, see published works by Pamila Gupta. As for the author's presumed mixed ancestry, we know his father and paternal grandparents were Goan. Little is known about his mother, but Goans tended to marry within the community.

belonging:[16]

O Pescador de Moçambique

Eu nasci em Moçambique,
de pais humildes provim,
a cor negra que eles tinham
é a cor que tenho em mim;

Sou pescador desde a infância
e no mar sempre voguei,
a pesca me dá sustento
nunca outro mister busquei.

Antes que o sol se levante
eis que junto à praia estou;
se ao repoiso marco as horas,
à preguiça não as dou;

Em frágil casquinha leve,
sempre longe do meu lar
ando entregue ao vento e às ondas
sem a morte recear.

Ter continuo a vida em risco
é triste coisa, não é?
mas do mar não teme as iras
quem em Deus depõe a fé!

Vou da Cabaceira às praias,
deixo perto Mussuril,
traje embora o céu de escuro
ou todo seja d'anil;

De Lumbo visito as águas
e assim vou até Sancul,
chego depois ao mar alto,
sopre o norte ou ruja o sul. [...]

The Fisherman of Mozambique

[I was born in Mozambique,
to humble parents,
the black skin they had
is the skin I own;

I have been a fisherman from childhood
and on the sea have I always sailed,
earning a life as a fisherman
no other work I ever sought.

Before the sun rises
here I am by the beach;
If I set a schedule on resting,
I do not do the same for idleness;

In a fragile, light boat,
always away from home
I follow the waves and the wind
without fearing death.

Constantly risking one's life
is a sad thing, is it not?
But you do not fear the wrath of the sea
if you trust in God!

I go from Cabaceira to the beaches,
leaving Mussuril nearby,
even if the skies are black
or enveloped in indigo hues;

I visit Lumbo waters
and I follow them to Sancul,
till I reach the high sea,
blown by either northern or southern winds. [...]]

Just as we considered that the poet's reference to race expresses his sense of belonging to Mozambique, we believe that the description of his maritime journey through several villages near the isle — Cabaceira, Mussuril, Lumbo, Sancul — situates geographically his lived experience, while underlining his emotional connection to the sea. This bond between the poet's voice and his birthplace will reappear in other texts, for example, *Cartas a uma Senhora*, published in *Revista Africana* ('1º Anno, Março de 1881, nº 1').

Another interesting aspect of Campos Oliveira's poetry is his keenness for satire, examples of which are to be found in poems like *A Uma Senhora Muito Feia* [To a very ugly lady], *Charada* [Charade], *Uns Versos* [A Few Lines]. This taste for satire reveals a thematic appropriation (and even a formal

---

[16] Cf. Ferreira, p. 111. All translations are our own unless otherwise indicated.

one) of poems by Nicolau Tolentino or Bocage, confirming his knowledge of Portuguese literature and its influence on his works.

Another point worth mentioning is that the most frequent theme across the poems written by the author is love, especially as it was idealized by late Romanticism, either as virginal and idyllic, lived through exacerbated emotions, or as a deadly fate, set among ruins, ghostly atmospheres and graveyards.

We conclude this part of our study by arguing that the poetry created by Campos Oliveira is designed after Portuguese and Goan literary models (the Goan dimension is addressed in the next section) and bears the influence of both metropolitan literature and its dislocated colonial appropriations. We also defend that this author's legacy stands as the first documented instance of literary expression in Portuguese to be published in Mozambican territory, specifically in the Island of Mozambique, the old capital city. On the one hand, contemporary acknowledgment of Oliveira's works sets the beginning of Mozambican literature, written by Mozambicans, far earlier than was thought, to the last decades of the nineteenth century. On the other hand, it is interesting to note that the birthplace of Mozambican literature — Mozambique Island — would become a key literary motif for Mozambique's postcolonial poetry by the end of the twentieth century, as if that specific place remained the symbolic keeper of national literary heritage.

Literary Collaborations in Goa

In the *Dicionário de Literatura Goesa,* by Aleixo Manuel da Costa (1997), Campos Oliveira is mentioned as 'natural de Moçambique, mas oriundo de Goa' [born in Mozambique, but of Goan descent].[17] The reference to family connections in Goa is important because it partially explains why Campos Oliveira was sent from Mozambique to Goa to pursue his formal education until he concluded high school (another motive would be the lack of equivalent educational facilities in Mozambique at the time). As mentioned above, according to Manuel Ferreira, Campos Oliveira lived in Goa until 1867,[18] the year he returned to Mozambique. In the previous section we established his legacy as a Mozambican poet, and in this part of the article we explore two other points in our argument: firstly, that Campos Oliveira's vision of the role of literary periodicals was defined according to the Goan model he had been in contact with; and secondly, that it was during his formative years in Goa that Campos Oliveira discovered the literary trends he would take with him from Goa to Mozambique.

In our view, Campos Oliveira's activities as editor and contributor to the leisure sections of the press are as important as his poetic legacy. His initiatives reveal that he acknowledged his role as a cultural intervenient and that he was aware of the possibilities that lay before literary magazines as instruments

---

[17] Aleixo Manuel da Costa, *Dicionário de Literatura Goesa* (Macau: Fundação Oriente, 1997), p. 6.
[18] Manuel Ferreira established this date because the texts published in 1867, in the periodical *Almanach das Lembranças* for 1867, are signed with reference to Mozambique (Ferreira, p. 40).

to educate public opinion and disseminate new ideas in society. But one cannot understand his vision for the mission of cultural periodicals without establishing how Goa's literary atmosphere influenced him. Hence, we will now turn our attention to Goa at the time Campos Oliveira lived there.

In Goa, in the second half of the nineteenth century, the circulation of the regular press, the yearly 'almanacs' and the proliferating literary magazines (even if the latter tended to be short-lived projects) was becoming more current, and the availability of all of these periodicals contributed to promoting the habit of reading as a form of leisure accessible to various members of a household (including women). In the case of Goa, one must also mention, for the sake of context, the parallel circulation of periodicals in Marathi and English, together with the circulation of the Goan press in Portuguese. Besides, we would underline the fact that Francisco Luís Gomes published the first novel written by a Goan in 1866 (*Os Brâmanes*), having met with a warm reception both in Lisbon, where Gomes was a member of the National Assembly, and in Goa. This detail gives the reader a glimpse of the relatively cosmopolitan life of Goan elites and testifies to the advanced maturing stage of a local literature in Portuguese.[19]

Several literary magazines were circulating in Goa at this time (the 1860s), especially *Ilustração Goana* (1864–66), which came to be considered one of the most solid and influential projects in the Goan literary milieu. Determined to take part in the lively atmosphere around him, Campos Oliveira, who also signed his works as JPS, joined the group of contributors who published texts in the pages of *Ilustração Goana*, even though he was quite young at the time (he would be seventeen or eighteen years old). Under the direction of J. Gonçalves (Luís Manuel Júlio Frederico Gonçalves, 1846–1896), the prolific director of that periodical, Campos Oliveira found more than a possibility for the publication of his works. He found in him an inspiring colleague who encouraged him to join forces and collaborate in other projects, such as the *Almanach Litterário* for the year of 1865.

Around the same time, Campos Oliveira was organizing almanacs on his own, and he must have met the expectations of his sponsors, for he went on to prepare the *Novo Almanach de Lembranças Luso-Indiano* for the years of 1864, 1865 and 1866. He also left dispersed poetry published in several Goan newspapers, such as *O Ultramar* (1859–1941), a newspaper from the city of Margão.

It is legitimate to consider that these experiences were essential to opening the mind of the young Oliveira to the dynamics of local cultural life, making him aware of the importance of the press as a means to bring about cultural development and the refinement of public cultural references. Moreover, by the 1860s, Campos Oliveira was already professional enough to adapt his creations

---

[19] For a postcolonial revisionary approach to Goan literature, see Joana Passos, *Literatura goesa em português nos séculos XIX e XX: perspectivas pós-coloniais e revisão crítica* (Ribeirão: Editora Húmus, 2012).

to the kind of periodical he was collaborating with. For example, *Ilustração Goana* was a periodical that convened most local talents. It published poetry, short stories, *feuilletons*, articles on European literature (listing a nation's most canonical authors), a monthly chronicle, and biographies of the most accomplished Goan personalities. In line with the standards of this literary magazine, Campos Oliveira selected his most elaborate compositions for the pages of *Ilustração Goana*.

By contrast, yearly almanacs were more amusing and didactic, publishing riddles and charades, side by side with practical information on hygiene, agriculture and health. Light poems were equally a favourite, as were legends or short tales. As both literary magazines and yearly almanacs were also sold by post, they could reach a rural reading audience, outside of the main towns. Most of the poems Campos Oliveira published in almanacs are more accessible, straightforward poetical creations, suggesting he was aware of the kind of composition best suited for each type of periodical (we provide examples below).

As a prose contributor to *Ilustração Goana*, Campos Oliveira wrote ten chronicles ('Chronicas do mês') on local events and news, and an embryonic short story. Clearly, his main contribution was poetic. Concerning his poetry, a very important point for our argument is that it was here, in the pages of *Ilustração Goana*, that Campos Oliveira started to explore the themes and tone of late Romantic poetry that he would later cultivate in Mozambique. The particular features of this literary trend would then become evidence of a literary influence that migrated from Goa to the literary circle on Mozambique Island. This is the reason why we said above that the first instance of a literary initiative in Mozambique was influenced not only by metropolitan models but also by Goan literature itself, as this was the closest case of a thriving writing community in Portuguese, and one which was connected to Mozambique by several administrative and affective bonds.

At this point, we provide a concrete example of the poetry we are referring to. We selected the poem *Não Crês?!...* [Don't you believe it?!...] as a typical example of the fashionable romantic poetry of the second half of the nineteenth century, usually addressed to a (mute) feminine character, and confessional in tone and theme:

Não Crês?!... *Don't you believe it?!...*

Quando vi-te á vez primeira
Tua imagem feiticeira
Me captivou,
E logo, desde esse dia
N' alma o fogo da poesia
Se me-ateou.

[When I first saw you
Your bewitching face
Seduced me,
And from that day onward
The fire of poetry in my soul
Was ignited.

Nas debeis cordas da lyra
Com fogo audaz, sem mentira,
Teus dons cantei,

In the fragile cords of my lyre
With daring fire, without lies,
I sang of your talents,

Do teu rosto tão fagueiro	And of your tender face
Um retrato verdadeiro	A true portrait
Tambem tracei.	Have I drawn.
Descrevi os meus amores,	I have told of my love
As hórridas, cruas dôres	And of the cruel pains
Que padeci,	I suffered,
Como cego te-adorava,	As I blindly adored you,
Como o peito se me-anceava	While my chest burned
Pensando em ti.	Thinking of you.
[...]	[...]
E tu, archanjo de Deus,	And you, my archangel from God,
Dizes que nos versos meus	You say you cannot believe
Não podes crer!...	my poems!...
Insistes que os trovadores	You insist troubadours
Phantasiam seus amores	Imagine their loves
Sem nunca os ter!	Without ever feeling them!
[...]	[...]
Um poeta nunca mente,	A poet never lies,
Tudo o que no peito sente	Everything his heart feels
Em versos diz.	He says in his lines.
Mentir! oh! isso é tão feio	Deceit! Oh! That is so ugly
Que, meu bem, devéras creio	That, my love, I truly believe
Jámais o-fiz.	I have never done it.]

Campos Oliveira, in *Ilustração Goana* (1866, pp. 11–12)[20]

In the remaining stanzas of the poem, the poetic voice repeatedly declares his love and the true nature of his feelings, trying to make his lady believe his suffering. But, simultaneously, the overdone insistence ('a poet never lies' / 'I have never [deceived]') suggests some self-awareness on the part of the poet, letting the performativity of his assigned role show through the verses, revealing some artifice, even if the feelings may be true. If one accepts this line of interpretation for the poem, one has to infer that Campos Oliveira is a subtle poet, less superficial than he may seem.

The poems published in *Ilustração Goana* usually keep to this standard, and, although Manuel Ferreira claims that some of those which had been originally published in that literary magazine were later republished in almanacs, that possibility does not negate our point; it merely tells of later republications that Campos Oliveira managed to secure. Yet again, if one reads the list of poems published by Campos Oliveira in *Ilustração Goana* and then compares it to the examples of poetry published in almanacs, compiled by Ferreira himself, the difference is obvious, not in terms of quality, but in terms of subject and composition. These other poems are less complex in content and less 'wordy' in tone, as if they were conceived for a less experienced and well-read public. Consider the following example:

[20] Later republished in *Almanach Popular* (1867, p. 41).

O Cravo e a Rosa	[The Carnation and the Rose
Disse o cravo à fresca rosa,	The carnation told the fresh rose,
'Consentes, ó linda flor,	'Would you allow, lovely flower,
Que eu te dê um terno beijo	That I give you a tender kiss
Em sinal do meu amor?'	As a token of my love?'
'Pois não — respondeu a rosa —	'Certainly you can — answered the rose —
Consinto sim, podes dar;	You can kiss me;
A quem assim tanto me adora	To one who adores me so,
Não no posso recusar.'	I cannot refuse it.'
E dizendo, envergonhada	And thus speaking, embarrassed
Ao cravo se aproximou,	She approached the carnation,
E este todo extasiado	Who, enraptured,
A bela amante beijou.	Kissed the loved one.
Oh! Se eu fosse n'esse instante	Oh! If I were in that instant
Aquele cravo amador,	That loving carnation,
E a linda virgem que adoro	And the beautiful virgin I love
Aquela rosa de amor!...	That lovely rose!...]

Campos Oliveira, *Almanach Popular 1867*, apud Manuel Ferreira (p. 97)

We believe that by comparing the two poems, it is possible to gain an insight into the way Campos Oliveira adjusted his writing to different kinds of publications, and this is important because it demonstrates that the young poet was acquiring skills to launch editorial projects tailored to the local publics he might aim at. It also proves the extent to which the immersion of Campos Oliveira in Goa's literary atmosphere was varied and complete.

Furthermore, both poems quoted above voice an elegant, respectful courtship, according to the social codes of the time. This choice of themes and the poet's attitude confirm our claims regarding the model of late Romanticism that Campos Oliveira was learning in Goa, and which he would pursue later on, when writing in Mozambique. Thus, in the next section of this article, we are going to explore examples of his work after he returned to his homeland. We will also take *Ilustração Goana* as the model to experiment with a comparative analysis based on the fragments of *Revista Africana* to which we had access, in order to determine if there are any noticeable resemblances between these two publications (although the Mozambican periodical appeared twenty years later). The aim is to seek evidence of cultural transit between different regions of the Indian Ocean.

Initiatives upon Returning to Mozambique

Campos Oliveira is one of the earliest examples of the transference of literary influences from Goa to Mozambique. There is ample evidence that the reverse would also be true, as Mozambique became a key literary theme in Goan literature in Portuguese in later decades. Thus, two literatures from different margins of the Indian Ocean were connected across the water, in a flow of cultural exchange that would bloom until the 1960s. Campos Oliveira can also be approached as an author and editor integrated in diasporic networks, in transit along different societies of the Indian Ocean. In this second case, he should be part of a possible transnational canon, or literary system, ensuing from south–south cultural cross-fertilization. In both cases, research on these figures in transit is innovative and necessary to complete the history of the literary archive.

It is now time to come full circle and consider in some detail the *Revista Africana*, which Campos Oliveira published after returning to Mozambique, and which was the most memorable of his achievements. Released in 1881, that monthly periodical for learning and leisure was both edited and owned by Campos Oliveira. We quote a passage from the introduction, where the author elaborates on the motives behind his initiative:

> Ahi vai para o campo das letras a *Revista Africana*. Hoje que a imprensa está disseminando, por toda a parte, incalculáveis melhoramentos abrindo as portas da civilização e do progresso; hoje que o culto das letras vai conquistando crescente apreço atê nas mais remotas plagas e em tódas as classes da sociedade; devemos crêr que não ha ninguem que desconheça quanto é util um periodico instructivo e ameno, principalmente num paiz como este em que são escassos os meios de leitura.
>
> Animados por este pensamento e confiados na protecção dos que não recusam prestar agasalho a empresas que, pela sua inquestionável utilidade concorrem em parte para um adiantamento de um paiz: ouzámos empreender a publicação deste periodico, cuja missão seria para nós de todo o ponto impossível cumprir, se não contássemos com o valioso auxílio de talentos robustos que de bom ânimo se prestaram a vir sentar-se connosco à meza do trabalho e a enriquecer as páginas d'este periódico com as suas lucubrações. Franqueamos, também, e de muito bom grado, as nossas columnas à mocidade estudiosa d'este paíz, declaramos desde já que por muito felizes nos daremos se conseguirmos arrancar da sombra talentos talvez proveitosos, inspirando-lhes o gosto da leitura e chamando-os a este entretinimento litterario, em que se aprende escrevendo e se escreve aprendendo.
>
> [Here you have the *African Magazine*, a periodical for the field of African writing. Currently, as the press is disseminating everywhere the great improvements of progress and civilization; nowadays that the cult of the arts is gaining momentum even in the most remote towns and among all the social classes; we believe nobody would question the advantages of an educative, leisure periodical, especially in a country where the opportunities for reading are not plentiful.

Encouraged by these thoughts, and trusting the protection of those who do not deny their support to enterprises that undoubtedly render a service to the improvement of a country, I dared to undertake the publication of this periodical, whose mission would be impossible to see through if we were not relying on the invaluable assistance and robust talent of all those who, in high spirits, were willing to share our working desk and contribute with their assistance to the pages of this periodical.

We wholeheartedly open our pages to the scholarly youth of this country, declaring our pride if we happen to provide young talents with the opportunity to step out from anonymity, summoning them to this literary forum, where you learn by writing and write by learning.]

Campos Oliveira, *Revista Africana*, no. 1, March 1881, p. 1

In the above quote from the 'Introdução' [Introduction] of the first issue of *Revista Africana*, Campos Oliveira mentions good examples of the role of the press 'everywhere'. Surely, the literary life he had witnessed in Goa is one of the examples (if not the main one) that motivated him to start an educative and entertaining periodical to enliven local cultural life on the Island of Mozambique. Thus, one may conclude that the creation of *Revista Africana*, with such a declaration of intentions, is an example of the transference of ideas from Goa to Mozambique.

Furthermore, he did remain a romantic poet in terms of aesthetic references and favourite themes, keeping in line with the literary trends he had been in contact with in his youth. Since we have quoted above an example of his romantic poetry, we will now explore an instance of his prose instead, providing an illustration of this other facet of his writing. We selected an excerpt of a 'Letter to a Lady', from page 1, issue 1 of *Revista Africana*:

Escrevo estas linhas na Cabaceira, sob as ramagens de duas robustas e copadas acácias, sentinellas permanentes postadas junto à porta principal da minha humilde e muito pequena vivenda. Vim hoje passar o dia que é feriado no campo. Eu amo desassombradamente o campo, e se não tivesse prendido o meu futuro numa repartição do estado, não me viam senão duas vezes, quando muito, em cada anno. Este inútil bulício da cidade produz em mim um aborrecimento que incommoda.

Como estou na Cabaceira, vou fallar a V. Exc.ª desta aldeola garrida e viridente, e porventura, a mais bonita da minha terra.

Eu creio que V. Exc.ª não se esqueceu de que tenho a mania de fazer versos e que por isso, gosto de tudo quanto é poético e romanesco. Soltemos pois as azas à poesia. Permitta-me que devaneie um pouco.

Ora imagine agora V. Exc.ª que está na Cabaceira; imagine que vai rompendo a manhã. Eu offereço-lhe o meu braço e peço-lhe que vamos dar um passeio.

[I write these lines from Cabaceira, under the branches of two robust, large acacias that stand as permanent guardians by the door of my humble and tiny villa. I came to spend the holy day in the countryside. I love the countryside passionately, and if I hadn't committed my future to a state department, you would see me in town twice a year at the most. The useless city hustle disturbs and bores me.

Since I am at Cabaceira, I am going to tell Your Excellency of this colourful and lush village, possibly the most beautiful of my land.

I believe Your Excellency has not forgotten that writing poetry is an obsession of mine, and consequently I like everything that is inspiring and romantic. Let us then give free rein to poetry. Allow me to daydream for a while.

Imagine that you are at Cabaceira; imagine it is dawn. I offer you my arm and invite you for a walk.]

> Campos Oliveira, 'Cartas a uma senhora', *Revista Africana*, no. 1, March 1881, page 1

In this letter, addressed to a Goan lady, one can recognize the typical romantic preference for solitude, the countryside, and the pleasure experienced by the poet in the contemplation of nature, features that confirm our claims regarding the transference of Romantic literary patterns to Mozambique. Moreover, the main objective of the letter seems to be a seduction game, which culminates with the invitation for a walk.

Another important characteristic of the excerpt quoted above is its representation of Mozambican landscape and geography, fulfilling the expected role of a traditional national literature, which is territorialized, embedded in a particular culture, territory and history.

In the fragments of the first issue of *Revista Africana* to which we had access, we noted that beyond the introduction or editorial[21] and the letter quoted above, it also comprised,

a) a short narrative ('Um conto oriental' [An Eastern Tale]);

b) an article on the Portuguese discoveries in Africa ('Notas sobre a história dos descobrimentos dos portuguezes em África');

c) poetry — Campos Oliveira signs the poem 'Dois Anjos' [Two Angels];

d) pieces of news (for example, on the discovery of the tomb of D. João Lencastre on the Island);

e) extracts from famous French and Portuguese writers;[22]

f) charades and riddles;

g) a review[23] of a book by Joaquim d'Almeida Cunha;

h) historical texts, such as *Provisão do Conselho Ultramarino da Camara de Moçambique expedida em 29 de Março de 1783*, under the rubric 'Antiqualhas'.

---

[21] This editorial from 1881 was reprinted in 1885.

[22] On page 6, one can even find an excerpt from an original by Alexandre Dumas (*Le Véloce*) under the title: 'De como um Zuavo vendeu o Calabouço do Regimento'.

[23] With the title 'Chronica', Campos Oliveira carries out a review of the book *Estudo acerca dos banianes, bothiás, parses, mouros, gentios e indígenas para cumprimento do que dispõe o arigo 8, parágrafo 1º do decreto de 18 de Novembro de 1869*, written by a Secretary of the Provincial Government, Joaquim d' Almeida Cunha.

All these rubrics are common to other literary periodicals of the time, but the publication of old historical documents evokes the influence of another famous periodical from Goa, the *Gabinete Literário das Fontaínhas* (1846–52), a cultural magazine that set the example for the practice of recovering old documents.

Another interesting conclusion from the analysis of the first issue of the magazine is that it is possible to identify at least two collaborators, namely Simeão de Oliveira, who published a long article entitled 'Vasco da Gama', and Alfredo Maya, who signed a text about the sea ('Quatro Mil Léguas por Mar'). The second issue (1º Anno, 1 Nov de 1885) confirms the collaboration of Simeão de Oliveira (with the text 'Escolas Manuaes', pp. 12, 13 and 14), and two other new names appear as contributors: Eduardo de Noronha, who translated a short story by Gustave Droz ('Uma Noite de Núpcias', p. 11) and F. Quintella d'Assis, who contributed with an epigram.

By comparing issues 1 and 2, we managed to establish that there was a sort of general structure with designated rubrics that was kept from issue to issue, although there was room for new contributions and ideas as well. For example, issue 2 features 'Escriptura de doação da Igreja do Mossuril' [the legal document concerning the donation of Mossuril church] (p. 14) under the rubric 'Antiqualhas'. Campos Oliveira in turn contributes to the second issue of the magazine with a poem, a chronicle, and an article on Camões.

From the detailed observations laid out above, we concluded that *Revista Africana* has some features of a literary magazine, publishing biographies of important personalities (such as Luíz de Camões), critical reviews of local publications, quotes and translations from canonical authors (e.g. Alexandre Dumas and Gustave Droz), as well as historical documents and articles related to the island's past. Moreover, all three issues we found at the Biblioteca Nacional de Portugal contain poetry and chronicles. However, the final section of both 1885 magazines resembles an almanac, on account of the publication of puzzles, charades, anecdotes and correspondence. In visual terms, *Revista Africana* is sober, with some black and white pictures of Camões and da Gama.

In his study on Campos Oliveira, Professor Manuel Ferreira established the missing link in nineteenth-century Mozambican literary history, before the canonical figures of the Albasini brothers and Rui de Noronha. With this article we have contributed to expanding and deepening knowledge regarding aspects of the works by Campos Oliveira and the influences he integrated in his creations. Besides, we have carried out a detailed critical analysis of *Revista Africana* (1881–85), a task that had yet to be achieved.

We believe Campos Oliveira may have been forgotten because his publications did not circulate. To be sure, only a small number of copies were issued, which would explain why a complete collection of the volumes of *Revista Africana* cannot be found anywhere. In addition, we think that a publication from the Island of Mozambique might not have circulated easily outside that circumscribed location. Furthermore, poems by Campos Oliveira remained scattered across several periodicals. They have been carefully compiled by historian António Sopa, who worked at the National Archive of Mozambique. Sopa is preparing a publication of Campos Oliveira's collected poems, to complement the article already published in the Mozambican journal *Arquivo* (1988, nº 4).

The change of the capital from Mozambique Island to the city of Lourenço Marques, in 1898, moved the cultural milieu away from the island. As a consequence, references that might have been important on the island were ultimately forgotten. Lastly, the press and the so-called 'almanac literature' have been marginalized by the critics, and it was only recently that such sources started to be revisited, receiving serious critical attention.

The comparative discussion between Goan periodicals and the noticeable influences of their models in the design and organization of *Revista Africana* also enabled this study to document the transference of a specific late-romantic literary culture from the periodical press of Goa to the Island of Mozambique, which was the capital of the territory at the time.

The Other (Hi)Stories: Diasporic Tides of the (Lusophone) Indian Ocean in *Skin* and *O Outro Pé da Sereia*

Kamila Krakowska Rodrigues

University of Leiden

The Indian Ocean's history of trade and migration offers insights into the global history of power relations and mobility. From a human historical perspective, the shores of Africa and Asia first met at the intersection of the ancient Arab, Indian and Swahili merchant routes, before the arrival of the European presence and the establishment of the transatlantic slave trade in the early modern era. As Isabel Hofmeyr points out in her seminal essay 'Universalizing the Indian Ocean', this interregional arena invites us to question facile dichotomies, to negotiate competing stories and to unwrap complex power hierarchies and dependencies, ultimately '[moving] us away from the simplicities of the resistant local and the dominating global and toward a historically deep archive of competing universalisms'.[1] In this scenario, we have to rethink key categories such as nation-state, diaspora, and religious universalisms as well as to break away from the Western model of modernity to rather engage with 'those formations of modernity that have taken shape in an archive of deep and layered existing social and intellectual traditions'.[2] Literary texts produced in the Indian Ocean world, as will be argued in this article, can be interpreted as critical responses to such — often fragmented, inaccessible, or even only imagined and non-existent — archives and can be read (following Maria Olaussen) as 'an exercise in understanding the structures that determine the relations of power'.[3] These 'multifaceted structures of power and dependence as well as the limitations of subject positions based on individual humanism'[4] are depicted in a particularly inspiring and thought-provoking way in novels that engage precisely with the historical connections between the Indian Ocean and the Atlantic worlds in the context of the slave trade and their legacy in the formation of identities in contemporary postcolonial and transnational societies.

---

[1] Isabel Hofmeyr, 'Universalizing the Indian Ocean', *PLMA*, 125.3 (2010), 721–29 (p. 722).
[2] Isabel Hofmeyr, 'The Black Atlantic Meets the Indian Ocean: Forging New Paradigms of Transnationalism for the Global South — Literary and Cultural Perspectives', *Social Dynamics: A Journal of African Studies*, 33.2 (2007), 3–32 (p. 13).
[3] Maria Olaussen, 'Archival Trajectories and Literary Voice in Indian Ocean Narratives of Slavery', in *Institutions of World Literature: Writing, Translation, Markets*, ed. by Stefan Helgesson and Pieter Vermeulen (London and New York: Routledge, 2016), pp. 109–25 (p. 109).
[4] Olaussen, 'Archival Trajectories', p. 113.

This article explores the ways in which storytelling is a crucial tool for remembering, re-enacting and rewriting of traumatic waves of displacement, in a cathartic process in which both the victims and the perpetrators can be given voice, by taking as case studies two contemporary novels written on opposite shores of the Indian Ocean. The 2001 novel *Skin* by Margaret Mascarenhas tells the story of a young journalist, US-born and raised, but of Goan descent, who returns to her paternal homeland to overcome a personal trauma. The 2006 novel *O Outro Pé da Sereia* by Mia Couto also presents a female protagonist who returns to her hometown after years of living in almost complete solitude in a nearby village in the Zambezi region of Mozambique. In the two novels, the protagonists Pagan and Mwadia need to delve into the history of the slave trade in the Indian Ocean to understand the tensions and fractures within their own families and within the communities they belong to. By listening, reading and narrating, the two characters engage in tracing and reconstructing the silent — and silenced — history of their families and of the free and forced migrations traversing the region across centuries. Symmetrically, *O Outro Pé* offers an intergenerational literary account of Indian Mozambicans while *Skin* portrays the virtually invisible black community in Goa. By analysing the two novels as mirror-images of one another within the framework of Indian Ocean Studies and Critical Archival Studies, this article will address transnational identity building in post-imperial and postcolonial contexts, in which the past seems to be a haunting presence.

The Archive on the Move

The framework of Critical Archival Studies allows us to understand the creative ways in which both *Skin* and *O Outro Pé* engage with historical and fictional records to capture — and to silence — the history of slavery in the Indian Ocean. As Terry Cook argues, the archive — seen as a concept, a practice and an institution — performs a double-edged role: it preserves as well as creates memory. However, remembrance is intertwined with oblivion and thus memory creation involves selecting certain records and certain stories while silencing others.[5] Critical Archival Studies addresses precisely the different tensions and fractures inherent in the records' selection, preservation and dissemination.

In this regard, the Queer/ed Archival Methodology proposed by Jamie Ann Lee offers a valuable framework to analyse the embodied narratives of the past intertwined in Mia Couto's and Margaret Mascarenhas's novels. The guiding principle behind this methodology is the acknowledgment of the ephemeral character of the archive. The concept of the archival body — which encompasses both the human bodies and the archives — allows the author 'to articulate the queer and the archival, two seemingly distinct and opposing constructs; one

---

[5] Terry Cook, 'Evidence, Memory, Identity, and Community: Four Shifting Archival Paradigms', *Archival Science*, 13 (2013), 95–120 (p. 101).

dynamic, the other held and preserved and, therefore, considered relatively static'.⁶ Such an approach opens up new conceptual perspectives that allow us to explore multiple, complementary, but also competing narratives emerging from the archival records. Importantly, Lee highlights that introducing the notion of the nomadic as an interpretative framework allows us to conceptualize the archival bodies as 'shifting sites of (un)becoming' and situate the collected stories as 'stories so far'.⁷ Unsettling the supposedly static archive is thus a critical praxis employed 'so that archival practices do not reproduce neocolonializing categories or further subjugating conditions'.⁸

However, when engaging with the notions of nomadic subjectivity and states of (un)becoming proposed in Queer/ed Archival Methodology, it is crucial not to overlook the power structures and dynamics inherent to mobility, whether the latter concerns the physical movement of the people and communities portrayed or whether it portrays the movement associated with the collection, reproduction and dissemination of stories. As Sheller and Urry argue in their proposal for the New Mobilities Paradigm, there is an urgent need to challenge the sedentary approaches still predominant in certain social science and humanities-based research which 'treats as normal stability, meaning, and place, and treats as abnormal distance, change, and placelessness',⁹ a clear preoccupation in Lee's methodological framework. However, Sheller and Urry also reject a certain grand narrative of mobility which celebrates nomadism without addressing explicitly the power structures that facilitate but also constrain mobility and change. Therefore, '[m]obilities cannot be described without attention to the necessary spatial, infrastructural and institutional moorings that configure and enable mobilities'.¹⁰ A comparative close reading of *Skin* and *O Outro Pé* will be a springboard to explore precisely the relation between mobility and materiality in narrating the Indian Ocean world's entangled histories of free and forced migrations.

Literary texts such as Couto's and Mascarenhas's novels open up a narrative space to engage with fragmentary records of a traumatic past and imagine the silenced, unheard voices. They can thus be read as artistic reproductions of 'impossible archival imaginaries', a concept explored by Anne J. Gilliland and Michelle Caswell to address human and ethical considerations related to the study of records that are unavailable, yet constitute sources of personal or public affect. Importantly,

---

⁶ Jamie Ann Lee, 'A Queer/ed Archival Methodology: Archival Bodies as Nomadic Subjects', *Journal of Critical Library and Archival Studies*, 1.2 (2017), 1–27 (p. 3).
⁷ Lee, 'A Queer/ed Archival Methodology', p. 5.
⁸ Lee, 'A Queer/ed Archival Methodology', p. 6.
⁹ Mimi Sheller and John Urry, 'The New Mobilities Paradigm', *Environment and Planning A*, 38 (2006), 207–26 (p. 208).
¹⁰ Kevin Hannam, Mimi Sheller and John Urry, 'Editorial: Mobilities, Immobilities and Moorings', *Mobilities*, 1.1 (2006), 1–22 (p. 3).

impossible archival imaginaries and the affect associated with the imagined records produced within those imaginaries, offer important affective counterbalances and sometimes resistance to dominant legal, bureaucratic, historical and forensic notions of evidence that so often fall short in explaining the capacity of records and archives to motivate, inspire, anger and traumatize.[11]

While including imagined records in the archival practice poses considerable challenges and disrupts the notions of evidence and authenticity,[12] fiction allows for the exploration of potential pluralist epistemologies that Gilliland and Caswell argue for in order to do justice to collective imaginaries rendered unheard and invisible. The affective dimension of such imagined records that the authors highlight works precisely as the organizing narrative thread in *Skin* and *O Outro Pé* which, as I will argue, are not so much novels about the history of the Indian Ocean *per se* but rather novels about (im)possibilities of unveiling and narrating its turbulent history. Their protagonists' endeavours to uncover the history of their families are not simply rooted in an enclosed past because 'the imagined record anchors and projects new possible futures, futures which are foreclosed in the absence of the material artifacts'.[13]

'Our mothers live under our skin'[14]

In Margaret Mascarenhas's *Skin*, Pagan's quest to unveil her family's history starts when she simply 'could write no more'.[15] An accomplished journalist and reporter, the young Goan-American woman suffers from post-traumatic stress disorder after her last assignment in a war-torn Angola. A sudden journey to India to meet her dying grandmother becomes an opportunity to listen to and discover the gaps and silences in the history of her own family, a painful yet healing process that allows her to recover her own voice, or rather to discover it for the first time. Indeed, there is no return to an earlier life. The epilogue depicts Pagan, who now divides her time between Goa and Brazil, the birthplace of her partner Xico, writing a novel 'seated at an old colonial teak desk in [her] mother's mud hut with a view of the sea'.[16] This transformation from a journalist who tries but fails to portray the 'unheard victims' of an armed conflict[17] into a novelist authoring a book suggestively entitled *White Lies* can be seen as an organizing narrative arc that questions the notion of fact-based evidence as a prerequisite of social justice.

---

[11] Anne J. Gilliland and Michelle Caswell, 'Records and their Imaginaries: Imagining the Impossible, Making Possible the Imagined', *Archival Science*, 16 (2016), 52–75 (pp. 55–56).
[12] Gilliland and Caswell, 'Records', p. 72.
[13] Gilliland and Caswell, 'Records', p. 71.
[14] Margaret Mascarenhas, *Skin* (Saligão: Goa 1556; Panjim: Broadway Publishing House, 2010), p. 241.
[15] Mascarenhas, *Skin*, p. 14.
[16] Mascarenhas, *Skin*, p. 261.
[17] Mascarenhas, *Skin*, p. 14.

Facts build the baseline of a story but, as different storytellers seem to point out throughout *Skin*'s plot, accuracy alone does not make a narrative meaningful and representative unless it also expresses and inspires affect. Pagan's psychological recovery starts when she feels that '[s]omething seems too pat' about the family's saga told by her aunt Livia,[18] and she asks the family's old maid Esperança to fill in the gaps. For Esperança, '[s]tories were medicine',[19] passed on from generation to generation, a source of knowledge and belonging, but also a motivation to embrace life and its different experiences. This movement between past and future, which Gilliland and Caswell identify as characteristic for imagined records,[20] is clearly illustrated in the episode in which Pagan as a child hides away in her room embarrassed by a rash on her face and Esperança tells her a story of a broken-hearted African oral poet who hides in his hut and stops singing the history of his tribe. Pagan quickly recovers when she realizes that her own story will be lost if she remains in hiding because, as Esperança warns her, 'As long as you are under the net, nothing interesting can happen to you, and so you will have no history to tell your children when you grow up.'[21] As stories are meant to be passed on to future generations, or — more precisely, within the narrative logic of *Skin* — to future generations along the maternal line, the act of storytelling is an act of love and affection.

Furthermore, Esperança's reflections on the nature of education invite the reader to question the very notion of truth and its relevance or applicability when accessing and representing the history of the Indian Ocean and African slavery there. Having accompanied Livia in her studies at the Sorbonne in the 1960s, the family's maid comes to the conclusion that official education offers only 'the colonial edition of history' while the 'true story always resides with the mothers [...] But that doesn't mean they always tell the truth.'[22] However, it seems that the notion of truth becomes limiting or even muzzling when trying to tell those stories that counterbalance official narratives. This is especially true concerning narratives implicated in the discourses on nation building, modernity and development in postcolonial contexts. Embellishment, as Saudade — Esperança's daughter and (as later revealed) Pagan's biological mother — puts it in her diary, can be a strategic narrative tool to allow stories to emerge, stories that matter, that hurt, that inspire:

> You see, there were stories within stories, myths, dreams, legends, skeletons in closets. Mothers and fathers who weren't. Green-eyed girls and cases of mistaken identity. A melting pot of histories, races, religions. People who owned other people. Points of view. Acts of courage, cowardice, deceit. And

---

[18] Mascarenhas, *Skin*, p. 31.
[19] Mascarenhas, *Skin*, p. 169.
[20] Gilliland and Caswell, 'Records', p. 71.
[21] Mascarenhas, *Skin*, p. 171.
[22] Mascarenhas, *Skin*, p. 47.

love — the heart of the matter. Hearts that mattered, shattered, scattered. Like shards from a broken mirror.[23]

Such a tension between facts and fiction, between knowledge and imagination, invites the reader to reflect on the silence of the archive and the (im)possible strategies to recognize and restore, if not whole stories, at least such silences. Indeed, as argued by R. Benedito Ferrão, '*Skin* centers the matrilinearity as an archive — a "place" of knowledge unrestricted by time and space as each successive generation of women continues to bear witness to the past.'[24] By exploring 'racialized and gendered dominance as contiguities of imperial and native patriarchies',[25] Mascarenhas's novel taps into the debates on the possibility to 'exceed or negotiate the constitutive limits of the archive'.[26] Saidiya Hartman's work on the (impossible) history of female slaves in the Atlantic is particularly relevant here. The author addresses precisely the obstacles in researching the 'irreparable violence of the Atlantic slave trade'[27] — which is unspoken and not captured by the official records — as well as in exploring the meaning behind trying to replicate or imagine such stories. Investigating the case of an enslaved woman murdered on board a slave ship, Hartman reflects:

> My account replicates the very order of violence that it writes against by placing yet another demand upon the girl, by requiring that her life be made useful or instructive, by finding in it a lesson for our future or a hope for history. We all know better. It is much too late for the accounts of death to prevent other deaths; and it is much too early for such scenes of death to halt other crimes. But in the meantime, in the space of the interval, between too late and too early, between the no longer and the not yet, our lives are coeval with the girl's in the as-yet-incomplete project of freedom. In the meantime, it is clear that her life and ours hang in the balance.[28]

Mascarenhas pointedly pictures the violence of trade in black bodies through the stories of Esperança's female ancestors, expanding the focus from the Atlantic to the Indian Ocean and attesting to the 'unrecognized African movement to Asia'.[29] The story of Perpetua, born into slavery after her mother had been raped by the head of the Miranda Flores family and cruelly tortured and murdered at the hand of her master and biological father, fictionalizes the unheard, unspoken and irreparable accounts of violence Hartman discusses in the Atlantic context. Ferrão offers an insightful close reading of Perpetua's death from the perspective of patriarchy and capitalism, with a special focus on the act of the cutting off the woman's breast and fashioning it into a purse:

---

[23] Mascarenhas, *Skin*, p. 6.
[24] R. Benedito Ferrão, 'The Other Black Ocean: Indo-Portuguese Slavery and Africanness Elsewhere in Margaret Mascarenhas's *Skin*', *Research in African Literatures*, 45.3 (2014), 27–47 (p. 29).
[25] Ferrão, 'The Other Black Ocean', p. 29.
[26] Saidiya Hartman, 'Venus in Two Acts', *Small Axe*, 26 (2016), 1–14 (p. 11).
[27] Hartman, 'Venus', p. 12.
[28] Hartman, 'Venus', p. 14.
[29] Shihan de Silva Jayasurija, 'Indian Ocean Crossings: Music of the Afro-Asian Diaspora', *African Diaspora*, 1.1/2 (2008), 135–54 (p. 139).

'The breast, a reminder of colonial and patriarchal desire, but also symbolic of women's ability to nurture life and transform their sexual power into maternity, is truncated into a capitalistic emblem of masculine greed and possessiveness.'[30]

Building upon this interpretation, I would argue that this episode brings forth also relevant ethical and epistemological considerations, tapping into the academic debates on 'impossible records'. Perpetua's death is represented within the logic of the narrative as a clearly traumatic (and traumatizing) event of the past which haunts future generations. Dehumanizing death literally annihilated Perpetua's voice and identity. Her dead body was unrecognizable since she was consumed by the spirit she had invoked to curse Dom Bernardo, her father.[31] After death, she was unable to reach her own daughter in dreams. While Pagan experiences recurring dreams of her biological mother, Saudade, Perpetua's daughter, Consolação, is deprived of the equivalent spiritual connection and anchoring. 'Sometimes, upon waking up in the morning, Consolação had the feeling that her mother had visited her in dreams but she could never recollect what she said, or whether she had spoken at all.'[32] This intergenerational silence, a haunting presence whose words cannot be captured, is a mechanism which creates a narrative that can 'embody life in words and at the same time respect what we cannot know',[33] which is what Hartman is arguing for.

Skin engages thus in a bilateral narrative movement between, on the one hand, imagining stories and voices of the Goan Siddis community — whose origins cannot be traced back 'to just one historical period or channel of migration'[34] — and on the other hand, disclosing the impossibility of writing a history that goes beyond the limitations of the archive. Pagan's story of being the descendant of an African enslaved woman, a Spanish Jesuit priest and a Goan Brahmani family who built their fortune on slave trade is just a 'story so far'.[35] Recalling, listening to and fictionalizing her own and her family's history — actually *White Lies* is a title of both Pagan's novel and one of the chapters in *Skin* — allows the protagonist to reflect on her own position as a racialized, gendered subject: the whitest girl in a Catholic boarding school in Goa, the brown one in a US public school; Katie's daughter, Saudade's daughter, a mother. By embodying all these stories, Pagan can be seen as an archival body herself, a body which is precisely transformative and shifting and thus challenging the supposedly static nature of the archive. Her transient body — travelling between continents and through storytelling, transiting between

---

[30] Ferrão, 'The Other Black Ocean', p. 41.
[31] Mascarenhas, *Skin*, p. 108.
[32] Mascarenhas, *Skin*, pp. 121–22.
[33] Hartman, 'Venus', p. 3.
[34] Mark Sebastian Pinto, 'The Forgotten Community, "the Siddis of Uttara Kannada": How the Portuguese Indian Ocean Slave Trade Produced a Community of Indians of African Descent', *InterDISCIPLINARY Journal of Portuguese Diaspora Studies*, 8 (2019), 165–88 (p. 166).
[35] Lee, 'A Queer/ed Archival Methodology', p. 5.

time periods — inscribes Goa in both the local and global socio-political and economic dynamics. Indeed, as argued by Joana Passos, *Skin* 'permite ao leitor uma visão de Goa ao mesmo tempo "de fora" e "de dentro", ou seja uma duplamente informada visão liminar, de fronteira' [offers the reader at the same time an 'outsider' and an 'insider' view of Goa, in other words a two-sided, liminal, border vision].[36] Importantly, this inbetween space of (un)becoming woven by *Skin*'s narrative threads is not unbounded. In the epilogue, Pagan reveals: 'I wear the sacred stone around my neck to remind myself from whence I came, where I am, and where I am going.'[37]

'Eis a nossa sina: esquecer para ter passado, mentir para ter destino'
[This is our fate: to forget to have a past, to lie to have a destiny][38]

While *Skin* explores the meaning and value behind storytelling practices, *O Outro Pé da Sereia* sets out from the idea of forgetting. Intertwining two parallel narratives, the novel fictionalizes the journey of a sixteenth-century historical figure, the Jesuit priest Dom Gonçalo da Silveira, from Goa to the Mutapa (or Monomotapa) empire, located in the vast territories along the Zambezi and Limpopo rivers in Southern Africa. Silveira's goal was to convert the African ruler, Muene Nogomo, to strengthen the Portuguese presence in the area. The mission was successful, but the priest was killed shortly after the king's baptism (apparently on the orders of the king himself, who was incited by Arab merchants afraid of losing their position in the regional commerce). This narrative is presented as a diary written by a priest accompanying Dom Gonçalo and is one of the fictional-historical artefacts which travel across the two narrative lines.

In fact, Silveira's journey engages in dialogue with the contemporary narrative at many levels. Just like the fictional diary, the other story line is set in the same region of the Zambezi valley and, as noted by Luís Madureira,[39] the two narratives are also linked by the presence of an *objet trouvé*, a wooden statue of the Virgin Mary. The artefact, according to the fictional account, was brought by Silveira as a gift for Muene Nogomo, and found together with the priest's remains by the novel's protagonist, Mwadia. This woman decides to return to her hometown, Vila Longe, to find a suitable place to keep the statue. On arriving, she learns that the inhabitants are preparing for a visit by two American scholars, Benjamin and Rosie Southman, who plan to do fieldwork on the memory of slavery in that region as well as propagate the ideas of an

---

[36] Joana Passos, 'Goa na diáspora e na literatura indiana em língua inglesa', *Via Atlântica*, 30 (2016), 85–98 (pp. 94–95).
[37] Mascarenhas, *Skin*, p. 261.
[38] Mia Couto, *O Outro Pé da Sereia* (Lisbon: Caminho, 2006), p. 75.
[39] Luís Madureira, 'Nation, Identity and Loss of Footing: Mia Couto's *O Outro Pé da Sereia* and the Question of Lusophone Postcolonialism', *Novel: A Forum on Fiction*, 41.2/3 (Spring/Summer 2008), 200–28 (p. 214).

NGO fighting 'Afro-pessimism'. This visit triggers a process of remembering, but also of reinventing Mozambican history and identity, when the local entrepreneurs try to present to the visitors an image of Africa that would match their expectations.

There is a considerable body of literature which focuses on the role of history and history writing in *O Outro Pé*. Elena Brugioni highlights that the relation between history and narrative is visible already in the graphic presentation of the original 2006 edition by Caminho: the white pages of the contemporary chapters contrast with the yellow paper of the sixteenth-century narrative, printed in a font imitating handwriting. Taking the apparently organic relation between story and history as her starting point, Brugioni argues that this novel is a story of post-coloniality which challenges the universal principles around such concepts as race, identity, history and tradition.[40] For Brugioni, the novel's originality lies precisely in the subversion of the dichotomy between the 'traditional' pre-colonial Africa and the 'modern' state created as a consequence of European colonization.[41] Jorge Valentim, too, finds the key to the interpretation of *O Outro Pé* in the interplay between the two story lines: it is 'a river of fiction' that opens up the dialogue between the contemporary and the historical narrative.[42] In particular, Mia Couto uses intrinsically fragmentary and imprecise information provided by the historical sources on the murder of priest Silveira to create a fictional account that '[d]os estilhaços da história, monta um outro novo espelho, sem imagens fixas, apenas com reflexos que podem ganhar os mais diversos formatos, dependendo do ponto de vista que se olha' [from the splinters of history assembles a new mirror, with no fixed images, only reflections that can take the most varied forms, depending on the point of view].[43]

Just as history writing is fragmented and imprecise, the same goes for collective memory. Forgetting seems to be depicted in the novel as an integral part of remembering: it is a shared, lived experience, symbolized by the imaginary of the Tree of Forgetting. The local people explain to the American visitors that they would ritually walk around the tree three times to forget where one comes from and who one's ancestors were. 'Tudo para se tornar recente, sem raiz, sem amarras' [Everything to become new, without roots, without moorings].[44] Interestingly, the symbolism of the tree brings forth the idea of rootedness on the one hand, and of vitality and rebirth on the other, connecting the past, the present and the future. Unrooting becomes thus a strategy of survival in a border land where the Zambezi river 'servia de refúgio

---

[40] Elena Brugioni, '*O Outro Pé da Sereia*: História(s) na Pós-colonialidade', *Luso-Brazilian Review*, 49.1 (2012), 46–62 (p. 48).
[41] Brugioni, 'História(s)', p. 50.
[42] Jorge Vicente Valentim, 'Entre mapas movediços e águas míticas: alguns jogos de espelho em *O Outro Pé da Sereia*, de Mia Couto', *Crítica Cultural*, 6.2 (2011), 367–92 (p. 373).
[43] Valentim, 'Entre mapas movediços', p. 376.
[44] Couto, *O Outro Pé*, p. 321.

e barreira para assaltos de estranhos e vizinhos, guerreiros ferozes e raptores de escravos' [served as a refuge from and barrier against attacks from strangers and neighbours, fierce warriors and slave stealers].[45]

Chandani Patel offers an insightful reading of the motif of forgetting woven in the narrative arguing that 'forgetting generates a new kind of life' for the characters who 'have no markers of race, religious affiliation, or national past with which to produce [a] shared identity'.[46] As a complement to Patel's interpretation that forgetting opens up a space for an alternative present (and future), I would argue that the overt ritualization of oblivion represented in the novel invites the reader to reconsider the contribution of the archive (which can document trauma and violence) to post-conflict reconciliation. According to Mia Couto, Mozambique became a nation 'not because we speak the same language or because we remember the same things, but because we forget the same things in the same way'.[47] However, *O Outro Pé* suggestively paints this forgotten, or rather unspoken, past as a haunting presence, in a similar manner to Perpetua's silent apparitions in *Skin*. In the chapters preceding the protagonist's journey back home, the river's waters turn red when touched by Mwadia's husband, Zero. The man's hand awakes the blood that 'já estava lá, adormecido no rio' [was already there, asleep in the river],[48] a testimony to centuries of fight and flight. The feeling that 'morre apenas a História, os mortos não se vão' [only History dies, the dead do not leave][49] — as expressed in the epigraph opening the first chapter, attributed to the town's barber — traverses the interconnected stories to culminate in Mwadia's vision of her family photos, photos which are only displayed to treasure the loved ones who passed away.[50] This ambivalent ending which makes the reader question the veracity of the plot within the narrative logic, opens up a liminal space in between presence and absence, storytelling and silence, where Mwadia can navigate and reposition herself within the narratives of the past in a dynamic relation between 'being' and 'becoming'.[51]

In this context, the idea of forgetting presented in *O Outro Pé* is not an act of erasure. It is rather a textual exploration of the limits and potential of the archive to engage with precisely these stories that 'motivate, inspire, anger and traumatize'[52] and that cannot be possibly moulded in any grand narrative

---

[45] Couto, *O Outro Pé*, p. 343.
[46] Chandani Patel, 'Goans, Oceans, and Intersections: Alter-Histories and Alternative Presents in Mia Couto's *O outro pé da sereia*', *Research in African Literatures*, 48.2 (2017), 94–111 (p. 105).
[47] Ana Mafalda Leite et al. (eds), 'Interview with Mia Couto', in *Speaking the Postcolonial Nation: Interviews from Angola and Mozambique* (Oxford: Peter Lang, 2014), pp. 173–98 (p. 178).
[48] Couto, *O Outro Pé*, p. 53.
[49] Couto, *O Outro Pé*, p. 15.
[50] Couto, *O Outro Pé*, p. 381.
[51] Stuart Hall, 'Cultural Identity and Diaspora', in *Colonial Discourse and Post-colonial Theory: A Reader*, ed. by Patrick Williams and Laura Chrisman (New York: Columbia University Press, 1994), pp. 222–37 (p. 225).
[52] Gilliland and Caswell, 'Records', pp. 55–56.

of (national) reconciliation. In this regard, Mwadia's trance sessions, enacted to give the American visitors a feeling of an 'authentic' Africa,[53] can be read as 'stories so far',[54] comparable to Saudade's 'embellished' diary in *Skin*. Mia Couto's protagonist reads historical records, including the fictional diary written by a missionary accompanying D. Gonçalo da Silveira, in order to compose her own story of arrivals, crossings and departures in an embodied performance where she 'se exibia de meter medo: olhos revirados, cabelos hirsutos, braços ondeando como se vogassem entre águas e nuvens' [showed herself off in a terrifying way: rolled-back eyes, shaggy hair, arms swaying as if sailing between the waters and the clouds].[55] Despite the scene being a theatrical performance to impress the guests (and as can be read in between the lines, to challenge tio Casuarino who had pressured Mwadia to participate in such a spectacle), the invented narrative, composed out of threads of historical records, allows Mwadia to engage in a meaningful way with her own and her spectators' nomadic subjectivity. By operating at the liminal (story)space between fact and imagination, Mwadia — like Pagan — becomes an archival body, dynamic, transitory, but still rooted in historical and lived experience. Her act of story(re)telling 'maintain[s] a level of unsettledness to leave translation and interpretation open',[56] something that Lee argues for in the framework of the Queer/ed Archival Methodology. On the other hand, just like Pagan's writings transiting in between the time-spaces of the Indian Ocean's fragmented, silenced contact zone, Mwadia's 'critical fabulations'[57] allow for an emotional and possibly cathartic engagement with the traumas anchored in the history of transoceanic forced and free migrations, still inscribed in this region's socio-political and cultural dynamics.

The tension inherent to the narratives of (un)becoming is further explored in *O Outro Pé* through the characters of diasporic identity such as the Afro-American couple but also Mwadia's Indian stepfather and aunt. The topic of cultural hybridity has been already addressed in several pieces of research. Carmen Tindó Secco connects the destabilization of Eurocentric approaches to African history in Couto's novel with the need to reclaim the hybrid character of Mozambican culture in the past and in the present.[58] This interpretation is in line with the reading by Nazir Can, who argues that the Indian imaginary in *O Outro Pé* constructs the topos of hybridism,[59] providing an insight into

---

[53] Couto, *O Outro Pé*, p. 276.
[54] Lee, 'A Queer/ed Archival Methodology', p. 5.
[55] Couto, *O Outro Pé*, p. 273.
[56] Lee, 'A Queer/ed Archival Methodology', p. 6.
[57] Hartman, 'Venus', p. 11.
[58] Carmen Tindó Secco, 'The Other Feet of History: A Reading of *Chorira* by Ungulani Ba Ka Khosa and *O Outro Pé da Sereia* by Mia Couto', in *Narrating the Postcolonial Nation*, ed. by Ana Mafalda Leite et al. (Oxford: Peter Lang, 2014), pp. 45–66 (p. 58).
[59] Nazir Can, 'Os lugares do indiano na literatura moçambicana', in *Passagens para o Índico: encontros brasileiros com a literatura moçambicana*, ed. by Rita Chaves and Tania Macêdo (Maputo: Marimbique, 2012), pp. 217–30 (p. 223).

a more fragmented and multidimensional national identity. From a different perspective, Chandani Patel argues that the novel 'positions its Goan characters at the centre of the alter-histories it writes into being here, alter-histories that force a reconsideration of the categories of both African and Indian diasporas and the ancestral origins on which they rely'.[60] Such a transnational framework is also adopted by Luís Madureira who reads the novel's core symbol, the title's 'siren', as a metaphor of 'hybrid articulations of cultural difference'.[61] This idea is explored in more depth by David Brookshaw who sees the multi-directional border crossings present in the novel as a call for Mozambican cultural pluralism and an appeal to global identities in general. He argues that Mia Couto's representation of Mozambican identity is intrinsically hybrid in the sense of creative instability, as opposed to the Lusotropicalist ideal of assimilation, elaborated by Brazilian scholar Gilberto Freyre and disseminated in the 1950s by Salazar's dictatorial regime as a justification for its colonial stance.[62]

These readings offer valuable insights into the dynamics of identity building in multicultural contexts with a special focus on diasporic communities, showing how fiction engages with the Indian Ocean's history in a way that challenges easy binarisms and universalisms.[63] Importantly, the stories of the Rodrigues siblings, Mwadia's aunt Luzmina and stepfather Jesustino, invite the reader to reconceptualize the role of affect in creating an archive that can potentially capture 'multifaceted structures of power and dependence'[64] that Olaussen considers as the central axis of the narratives of/in the Indian Ocean world as well as 'turn impossible archival imaginaries into possibilities'.[65] The descendants of a Brahmani family of slave traders, Jesustino and Luzmina need to navigate within the social hierarchies constructed by the race-oriented discourse of the Portuguese colonial regime, where the Indian community occupied a rather ambivalent position, one which persisted post-independence, as evidenced by Thomaz and Nascimento.[66]

Jesustino is deeply hurt at being excluded from the interviews planned by the Southmans for not fitting into the clear-cut category of a 'true' African, a dialectic act replicating the 'comic classificatory and subclassificatory census boxes entitled "Other" conceal[ing] all real-life anomalies by a splendid bureaucratic trompe l'oeil'.[67] Jesustino clearly refuses any definitive classification when he

[60] Patel, 'Goans', p. 101.
[61] Madureira, 'Nation', p. 223.
[62] David Brookshaw, 'Indianos e o Índico: o pós-colonialismo transoceânico e internacional em O Outro Pé da Sereia de Mia Couto', in Moçambique: das palavras escritas, ed. by Margarida Calafate Ribeiro and Maria Paula Meneses (Porto: Afrontamento, 2008), pp. 129–39 (pp. 138–39).
[63] See Hofmeyr, 'Universalizing', p. 722.
[64] Olaussen, 'Archival Trajectories', p. 113.
[65] Gilliland and Caswell, 'Records', p. 73.
[66] Oscar Ribeiro Thomaz and Sebastião Nascimento, 'Nem Rodésia, nem Congo: Moçambique e os dias do fim das comunidades de origem europeia e asiática', in Os outros da colonização: ensaios sobre o colonialismo tardio em Moçambique, ed. by Cláudia Castelo et al. (Lisbon: ICS, 2012), pp. 315–39.
[67] Benedict Anderson, Imagined Communities: Reflections on the Origin and Spread of Nationalism

confesses to his stepdaughter that he is changing his race[68] and recurrently and deliberately abandons a fundamental mark of his identity: his name.[69] Such a display of discontinuity in the identity texture may be read in the context of the destructive impact of emotional exile. Édouard Glissant introduces a distinction between the concepts of exile and errantry precisely to pinpoint different effects of travels away from our emotional homelands. He argues: 'Whereas exile may erode one's sense of identity, the thought of errantry — the thought of that which relates — usually reinforces this sense of identity.'[70] Jesustino's annual baptisms do not add new components to a vibrant, multidimensional identity, as if in a romanticized nomadic imaginary, but simply cover up a hurtful void, a sense of longing for a space of his own. Despite feeling much more affinity with his African upbringing than with his Goan descent, the tailor is clearly exiled in between the shores of the Indian Ocean. He ends up telling his story to Rosie Southman when the woman comes to him in distress — 'naquele estado de alma, uma rodilha de desespero, balbuciando um rosário de lamentos' [in that state of mind, in despair, babbling a rosary of complaints][71] — after meeting the local postman, Zeca, for whom she has deep feelings. Jesustino wants to share his story but can only be heard when the interlocutor is ready and able to engage with feelings and emotions, with traumas and taboos.

The man's story is inseparable from the story of his sister Luzmina. It is a story of love, submerged, forbidden, accomplished, and finally rejected. The young woman supposedly falls in love with Zeca. However, she never declares her feelings because she does not consider him an appropriate match, both belonging as they do to subaltern groups in the colonial society as represented by Mia Couto, yet set apart from them. Luzmina thus keeps longing for a Goan Prince Charming who would be of 'adequada casta, estrato e geração' [suitable caste, status and upbringing][72] and her unwillingness to look for a suitor among the local men is explained either by her loyalty to the Indian social caste system or by her mystical and almost fanatical religious beliefs. Such an inflexible adherence to traditional Goan values could be read as the anchor upon which Luzmina desperately tries to construct her identity. Her personality seems though to be on the verge of disintegration, as shown by her later drastic behavioural changes. She engages in an incestuous relationship with her brother — in fact, the only inhabitant of Vila Longe of an equal social status — and, when later rejected, she publicly declares that she would be an excellent whore and become the patron saint of the prostitutes.[73] This chain of events is triggered by Jesustino discovering a love letter, a symbol of evidence, a proof to

(London: Verso, 1991), p. 184.
[68] Couto, O Outro Pé, p. 110.
[69] Couto, O Outro Pé, p. 83.
[70] Édouard Glissant, Poetics of Relation, trans. by Betsy Wings (Ann Arbor: University of Michigan Press, 2006), p. 20.
[71] Couto, O Outro Pé, p. 256.
[72] Couto, O Outro Pé, p. 257.
[73] Couto, O Outro Pé, p. 88.

be archived and documented. Importantly, the letter is not addressed to a real postal address but to 'a terra dos milagres' [the land of miracles],[74] showcasing Luzmina's dream of writing up an alternative present and future. 'Não é a carta que tem erros. É a vida, mano' [It's not the letter that contains mistakes. It's life, brother],[75] she declares. As 'the imagined record instantiates collective aspiration for not just what was, but what is and what will be possible',[76] Luzmina's visits to the post office, where she buys stamps for invented destinations, represent an urge to draw new trajectories of connection and contact that could circumvent the social and racial barriers constraining social mobility and relations. Transiting between facts and imagination, between sanity and delusion, Luzmina embodies competing stories of belonging and affect that escape traditional archival notions of evidence, veracity and stability to explore in the realm of fiction 'multiply-situated subjectivities' whose '[p]ast, present, and future intersect, overlap, and become the other'.[77]

The Other (Hi)Stories in the Indian Ocean

The history of the slave trade is still haunting the communities which came into being as a result of waves of displacement traversing the Indian Ocean and extending beyond its waters towards the Atlantic. Silenced, forgotten, and to a great extent inaccessible. Yet storytelling, in its momentary, performative nature, proves to be a critical tool for remembering, re-enacting and rewriting of such a traumatic past in ways that do not claim to present a definitive, universal truth, but rather try to engage with emotions and feelings triggered by such 'impossible archival imaginaries'.[78] As *Skin* and *O Outro Pé da Sereia* exemplify in their captivating and inspiring narratives, literature opens up thus a possibility for an alternative form of remembering that operates at the liminal space between representing and exploring the unspoken, the undepictable. Importantly, the stories that Pagan and Mwadia (re)create for themselves and their respective families are not accomplished, closed testimonies about a past that is made accessible and classifiable but rather 'stories so far'.[79] They are momentary, transient records that challenge both the universalisms implicated in processes of identity negotiation as well as the very nature of the archive. Both novels position the female body as the object of the exercise of power but also as a key agent in keeping or, in fact, recreating the memory of exploitation, abuse and resistance, in a way that writes history 'with and against the archive'.[80] Just like the postcolonial migratory texture of the Indian Ocean itself, Pagan and Mwadia, as fictional, female archival bodies that navigate through its history, bear witness to stories that matter.

[74] Couto, *O Outro Pé*, p. 259.
[75] Couto, *O Outro Pé*, p. 261.
[76] Gilliland and Caswell, 'Records', p. 71.
[77] Lee, 'A Queer/ed Archival Methodology', p. 7.
[78] Gilliland and Caswell, 'Records', p. 55.
[79] Lee, 'A Queer/ed Archival Methodology', p. 5.
[80] Hartman, 'Venus', p. 12.

Enchanted Things to Narrate the Oceans: João Paulo Borges Coelho and Luís Cardoso

JESSICA FALCONI

*CEsA — Center for African and Development Studies,
ISEG, University of Lisbon*

Introduction

One of the research strands of the NILUS project concerns the representations of elements of material culture in written and visual narratives related to the territories formerly colonized by Portugal in the Indian Ocean. The project aimed to develop previous considerations concerning the recurrent presence, in Mozambican poetry, of concrete forms associated with the material culture and imaginary of the Indian Ocean, thus functioning as metonymies of this universe (e.g. vessels, spices, precious stones). The present article seeks to provide a further contribution to that research strand, by addressing contemporary narratives from/about Mozambique and East Timor in order to investigate the role of material culture and materiality in the act of narrating and remembering, as this aspect is ripe with relevant meanings. The article addresses the short story 'O pano encantado' [The Enchanted Cloth] (2005) by João Paulo Borges Coelho (JPBC) and the novel *Requiem para o navegador solitário* [Requiem for the Solitary Sailor] (2007) by Luís Cardoso (LC), to show that summoning material culture and materiality constitutes, for both writers, a means of narrating and remembering the oceans from two insular spaces — the Island of Mozambique and the Island of Timor, respectively.

The analysis of these narratives combines reflections developed within Indian Ocean Studies and other perspectives which, in recent decades, have guided the study of materiality in various fields, including literary, visual and artistic representations. I refer in particular to the concept of material culture, which has a long history mainly in anthropology, archaeology and sociology, and is now an eclectic and transdisciplinary field, upon which diverse perspectives and methodologies converge.[1] Despite their heterogeneity, conceptualizations of material culture assume that material forms do not exist in a sphere separate from that of individuals, but that both constitute each other. For the specific purposes of this article, it is worth noting that the term encompasses a multiplicity of aspects of the material world that manifest themselves in cultural forms and artefacts — e.g. objects, food, buildings

---

[1] Chris Tilley et al. (eds), *Handbook of Material Culture* (London: Sage, 2006).

— while also hinting at the relationships that individuals and social groups establish with things through consumption, use, circulation, and exchange.[2] In other words, the notion of material culture carries the relational and social nature of things, emerging as the interface of relations between subjects and objects, also due to their metaphorical, symbolic, and mediating power.[3] The elements of culture materialize ideas, values, emotions, memories and identities, having the power to perpetuate, legitimize or transform these same ideas, values, etc. This power has also been explored in the field of literary and cultural studies, mostly in the analysis of English, French and American literatures, focusing on topics such as industrialization and mass culture, antiques and collectibles, and the circulation of goods between metropolises and colonies. Among the most recent developments, there are also perspectives focused on the relevance of material forms, such as thing theory,[4] based on the distinction between objects and things, and material ecocriticism,[5] with the aim of highlighting and analysing the agentivity of matter and the nonhuman. The mediating role of material forms has also become central to the analysis of narrative practices and the production of memory,[6] since material culture, thus understood, carries memories and bears witness to relationships, incorporating individual and collective memories, and evoking not only the local dimension of culture but also global connections.

These aspects and perspectives are especially relevant to the geographical and cultural context of the narratives to be addressed in this article, since material culture and materiality permeate, on a transdisciplinary level, many approaches to the Indian Ocean. The material dimension, regarded from the outset as a focus on the production, exchange, circulation and consumption of commodities, has emerged in historiography as a structuring axis of the identity of this ocean. For Chaudhuri, long-distance trade and the circulation of commodities provided the main basis for the construction of the historical unity of the Indian Ocean.[7] These were considered dominant forms of connection between the various shores of this ocean's sphere of influence.[8]

Pearson refers to this aspect in the introduction to his history of the Indian Ocean, expressing concern about the 'excess' of materiality present in Braudel's focus on the Mediterranean, as well as in the historiography of the Indian Ocean. Pearson proposes a different approach for this ocean:

---

[2] Daniel Miller, 'Consumo como cultura material', *Horizontes Antropológicos*, 13.28 (2007), 33–63.
[3] Chris Tilley, *Metaphor and Material Culture* (Oxford: Blackwell, 2008).
[4] Bill Brown, 'Thing Theory', *Critical Inquiry*, 28.1 (2001), 1–22.
[5] Serenella Iovino and Serpil Oppermann, 'Material Ecocriticism: Materiality, Agency, and Models of Narrativity', *Ecozon@*, 3.1 (2012), 75–91.
[6] Andrew Jones, *Memory and Material Culture* (Cambridge: Cambridge University Press, 2007).
[7] Kirti N. Chaudhuri, *Trade and Civilisation in the Indian Ocean* (Cambridge: Cambridge University Press, 1985); *Asia before Europe: Economy and Civilisation of the Indian Ocean* (Cambridge: Cambridge University Press, 1990).
[8] Kenneth McPherson, *The Indian Ocean: A History of People and the Sea* (New York: Oxford University Press, 1993).

> I want to avoid the concentration on the material, which characterises Braudel, and most books on the Indian Ocean. [...] I aim to describe both material and mental frameworks. [...] With all due deference, too many previous works have been almost entirely histories of trade, and especially European trade, rather than of the ocean. I want lots of connections, the ocean acting as a transmitter for disease, religion, tourists, goods, information, not just pepper and cotton cloths.[9]

Pearson structures the history of the Indian Ocean in such a way as to combine material aspects and human action and imagination; natural features and ideas; commercial and cultural exchanges, highlighting connections that took place along south–south axes and between multiple orients. The material and natural elements of the 'deep structure' of the Indian Ocean are connected to coastal societies, port cities, the voyages of sailors, merchants, and pilgrims, which in turn are illuminated by the focus on vessels and the cultures of navigation. Thus, to historicize the Indian Ocean means to connect the material and the immaterial; the human and the non-human, describing the ways in which these dimensions have intermeshed along the many seas and coastlines of the Indian Ocean: 'the Mozambique Channel, Red Sea, Gulf of Aden, Arabian Sea, Persian Gulf, Gulf of Oman, Bay of Bengal, Andaman Sea, Strait of Melaka, and the Laccadive Sea'.[10]

In a similar vein, Bose states that 'the overemphasis on trade has tended to obscure much else that went along with it, especially the flow of ideas and culture'.[11] Like others, Bose contributes to the construction of the Indian Ocean as a unit of analysis, exploring the role of Asian capital and labour, but also the ideas of universalism and poetry. Alpers, for his part, explores the declensions of Islam on the Swahili coast as connecting factors and distinctive cultural matrices of the Indian Ocean.[12] In sum, the vast historiography of the Indian Ocean[13] has disputed hierarchies, decentring units and perspectives previously held as hegemonic (the centrality of India, the marginalization of Africa, or the dominant focus on trade), calling into question reified and sometimes orientalist representations, undoing the narratives of an Indian Ocean crossed only by caravels and spices, to paraphrase Pearson. As summarized by Hofmeyr, 'if the Indian Ocean operates or has operated as a network, its unity resides in a myriad of factors: trade, capital, religion, war, pilgrims, ports, ships, slaves, indentured workers, clerics, sailors, creditors and commodities'.[14]

---

[9] Michael N. Pearson, *The Indian Ocean* (London and New York: Routledge, 2003), pp. 9–10.
[10] Pearson, *The Indian Ocean*, p. 16.
[11] Sugata Bose, *A Hundred Horizons: The Indian Ocean in the Age of Global Empire* (London and Cambridge, MA: Harvard University Press, 2006), p. 11.
[12] Edward Alpers, *The Indian Ocean in World History* (New York: Oxford University Press, 2014).
[13] Mark Vink, 'Indian Ocean Studies and the "new thalassology"', *Journal of Global History*, 2 (2007) 41–62.
[14] Isabel Hofmeyr, 'The Black Atlantic Meets the Indian Ocean: Forging New Paradigms of Transnationalism for the Global South — Literary and Cultural Perspectives', *Social Dynamics: A Journal of African Studies*, 33.2 (2007), 3–32 (p. 13).

However, in literary, cultural and anthropological studies focusing on the Indian Ocean there is a renewed investment in the material dimension and the 'natural logics' of the Indian Ocean,[15] in an attempt to view it as a material reality, grounded upon constitutive relations — human–nonhuman; natural–social; geological–cultural. From this perspective, echoing the multiple connections sought by Pearson, Muecke approaches the Indian Ocean as 'A natural-cultural continuum of connections. Each story, artifact, or flying carpet carries a bit of cultural value which, if you follow a zigzag path of associations is linked to natural things and beings'.[16] Samuelson elaborates on the notions of 'coastal form' and 'littoral literature', regarding the coast as a material and epistemological location to analyse and systematize Indian Ocean literary narratives, as well as to blur the national, regional or continental boundaries that traditionally compartmentalize the studies of literatures originating from this ocean.[17]

Aware of the complex balance between the excess of materiality in historiography and the call of cultural studies for greater engagement with it, I will seek to reflect on these issues by addressing the declensions of material culture and materiality in the chosen narratives. In these narratives, 'things' are closely linked to the construction of subjectivity and the identity of the characters, thus functioning as a junction between the material and human dimensions of the Indian Ocean. Starting from the assumption according to which 'Thinking through things [...] is critical to thinking through the Indian Ocean',[18] JPBC's short story draws attention to the creative use and deviation of material culture already in its title, referring to a special object ('The Enchanted Cloth'). In LC's novel, material transactions define the driving force of the narrative, and one object in particular helps to build the protagonist's identity. Thus, the present article aims to examine aspects that, in the light of the outlined framework, are eminently theoretical and thematic, potentially distinctive of a corpus of contemporary Indian Ocean narratives — a corpus that, to paraphrase Muecke,[19] has yet to be invented and to which the 'Lusophone' Indian Ocean narratives[20] contribute in a peculiar and evidentiary way. With few exceptions, such narratives thematize in a less direct manner the key topics of Indian Ocean conceptualization — i.e. migration, diaspora,

---

[15] Devleena Gosh and Stephen Muecke, 'Natural Logics of the Indian Ocean', *Cultural Studies Review*, 12.1 (2006), 118–31.
[16] Stephen Muecke, 'Fabulation: Flying Carpets and Artful Politics in the Indian Ocean', in *Indian Ocean Studies: Cultural, Social and Political Perspectives*, ed. by Shanti Moorthy and Ashraf Jamal (New York: Routledge, 2010), pp. 32–44 (p. 39).
[17] Meg Samuelson, 'Coastal Form: Amphibian Positions, Wider Worlds, and Planetary Horizons on the African Indian Ocean Littoral', *Comparative Literature*, 69.1 (2017), 16–24.
[18] Meg Samuelson, 'Narrative Cartographies, "Beautiful Things" and Littoral States in Abdulrazak Gurnah's *By the Sea*', *English Studies in Africa*, 56.1 (2013), 78–90 (p. 83).
[19] Muecke, 'Fabulation', p. 33.
[20] The adjective Lusophone is used here to denote a distinct experience of historical and cultural integration in the Indian Ocean, marked by the Portuguese colonization of the area.

forced labour, slave trade, hybridization, creolization, coolitude, etc. Therefore, following in the trail blazed by JPBC, they require the collection of 'evidence' and traces.[21]

Of Beautiful Cloths and Bridges, on the Island of Mozambique

'The Enchanted Cloth' is the first text of *Índicos Indícios*, a collection of short stories in two volumes — *Setentrião* and *Meridião* — that simultaneously constitutes a collection of traces and a coastal literary project. Set along the extensive Mozambican coastline, the narratives included in this collection map places, stories, and imaginaries, as announced in the preface:

> The Indian Ocean wets, one by one, the approximately two thousand five hundred kilometres of the Mozambican coast — a considerable stretch. Even larger if we consider the countless islands scattered along that coast. And much, much larger if we take into account the stories that this simple fact has nourished in the imagination of the present and over the long time that has elapsed.[22]

Pointing to 'natural logics' and the historical and imaginary dimension, JPBC proposes a chronotopic configuration of the coast, attempting to rethink Mozambique in coastal and insular terms and to incorporate imaginaries that transcend the nation-state. The bidirectional nature of the connection between Mozambique and the Indian Ocean emerges between water and land, sea and coast: if the Indian Ocean wets and shapes the Mozambican coast, it in turn acts on the sea, changing its colour and making it 'so often drab, tinged by everything that this coast lets escape through its liquid veins — lands and branches, memories and the drowned, plots and searches — that open themselves there to fertilize it'.[23] This suggests a dynamic relationship that is as much material and natural as it is cultural and historical. JPBC's stories map territories and itineraries of marginal subjects, protagonists of stories that have not been written but are embedded in the coastal folds and insular patches of the Indian Ocean.

The short story under analysis points to a material element right in the title and is set on the Island of Mozambique, a former focal point in the 'monsoon system', connecting northern Mozambique to the commercial, religious, and cultural circuits and networks of the Indian Ocean. Before introducing the two protagonists — the young tailor Jamal and Mr Rashid, owner of the tailor's shop — the narrator stops at the bridge that connects the Island to the mainland:

---

[21] Jessica Falconi, 'The Lusophone Space and the Indian Ocean: Towards New Cultural Cartographies', in *Revisiting Centres and Peripheries in Iberian Studies*, ed. by Mark Gant (Newcastle upon Tyne: Cambridge Scholar Publishing, 2019), pp. 397–409.

[22] João Paulo Borges Coelho, *Índicos Indícios*, I: *Setentrião* (Lisbon: Caminho, 2005), p. 9 (all translations are my own, unless otherwise indicated).

[23] Ibid.

> One has to cross the bridge to get to Mozambique Island. A narrow, metal, almost endless bridge that takes us from the mainland to the other side. As always, there are those who view the island warily, and others for whom it is the center of the world, and who regard the other side as wilderness.
>
> Whatever the case, and no matter what each one calls it, it is the bridge that contains all the mystery, for, by joining the two sides, it also makes us remember we are separated. Without a bridge, it would be a whole world in itself; with it, the Island became an island, a closed space that one can only enter or leave by crossing the bridge.[24]

Thus, before addressing the representation of the conflict between the characters, generated by their adherence to two distinct and incompatible versions of Islam, I will literally dwell on the bridge and its metaphorical ramifications. According to Can, the 'bridge' as a 'political and literary place' plays a special role in JPBC's work.[25] Indeed, through a survey of the occurrences of the bridge in the author's novels, Can records the literal materialization of this element, its reiterated absence, and also its personification, defining the — literal and metaphorical — bridge as an 'affective matrix' and a tool to 'reflect upon the division that plagues the country'.[26] Can further addresses the literal reference to the bridge in the short story under analysis, interpreting it as yet another occurrence of the author's 'disenchanted vision', since, given the conflicts portrayed in the text, the bridge does not materialize the union.[27] While I agree with this interpretation, I believe that pondering some aspects related to the literality and materiality of the bridge, in an extraliterary perspective, allows us to shed light on other meanings and broaden the metaphorical interpretation of this element, also taking into account the narrator's emphasis on the mystery that lies in it. In fact, from the perspective of space, the bridge is the quintessential mediating and relational element, and is associated by the narrator with time through allusion to remembrance. Moreover, as the narrator advises, 'on this island, [...] the relationships established between things and time are extremely mysterious'.[28] Therefore, the bridge is also a mediator between eras, conjuring up the separation, or in other words, the time when the Island was 'a world apart'. This may correspond to the phase when the Island was more attuned to the ocean than to the continent, that is, the long history of the integration of this location into the 'arena of economic and cultural interaction' of the Indian Ocean.[29] As for the literal and material bridge, it goes back to the time

---

[24] João Paulo Borges Coelho, 'The Enchanted Cloth', trans. by David Brookshaw, in *A Companion to João Paulo Borges Coelho: Rewriting the (Post)Colonial Remains*, ed. by Elena Brugioni, Orlando Grossegesse and Paulo de Medeiros, 2nd edn (Oxford: Peter Lang, 2020), pp. 11–35 (p. 11).
[25] Nazir Can, 'Entre ética e estética: as pontes de João Paulo Borges Coelho', in *Visitas a João Paulo Borges Coelho: leituras, diálogos e futuros*, ed. by Sheila Khan et al. (Lisbon: Colibri, 2017), pp. 53–74 (p. 53).
[26] Can, 'Entre ética e estética', p. 54.
[27] Can, 'Entre ética e estética', p. 70.
[28] Coelho, 'The Enchanted Cloth', p. 14.
[29] Bose, *A Hundred Horizons*, p. 15.

of the so-called late colonialism, conceptualized by more recent historiography as a 'specific historical period and process',[30] and coinciding roughly with the time frame spanning from the end of the Second World War to the formal constitution of the independent states. In the case of Mozambique, this is a phase that saw a new impulse of the colonial government in the development of territorial integration through investment in the improvement of transport, roads and communication systems,[31] and, more broadly, of colonial built environment, whose legacies and traces surface repeatedly in JPBC's work. Think, for example, of another short story in the same collection, dedicated to the Grand Hotel da Beira, built and opened in the 1950s in the Ponta Gêa neighbourhood, which in turn was reclaimed as a place of memory in the author's last book. In short, it is during this phase that 'colonial society becomes more complex and effectively distances itself from the Metropolis'.[32]

Designed in 1962 and inaugurated in 1967, the bridge materialized the attempt to revert the process of decadence faced by the Island, which was losing more and more centrality in the economic life of the colony to other ports on the coast, due in part to poor infrastructure.[33] Ever since the colony moved its capital to Lourenço Marques in 1897, the Island had been slowly transitioning from a focal point in the inter-regional arena of the Indian Ocean to a peripheral location, which the construction of the Mozambican nation from the south would consolidate after independence.

This late-colonial period materialized by the bridge is embedded in the text through the memories of Mr Rashid's character. Strongly attached to the colonial past, the owner of the tailor's shop dives into colonial nostalgia recalling other times of his commercial activity, marked by the abundance of textiles from India: 'worsted or tweed, cashmere, silk and cotton velvets, fine and coarse linen, hemp, muslins and printed cottons, tulle and even blackman's-fabric, made from the purest Daman cotton for our poorest customers'.[34] This activity is linked to complicity with the colonial power in the proud memory of a suit made for Governor Arantes de Oliveira, Minister of Public Works (1954–67) and Governor General of Mozambique (1970–72). When commenting on the name of his own store — 'Alfaiataria 2000', although no sign mentions it — Mr Rashid also alludes to the projection of the movie *2001: A Space Odyssey* (1968) in the Nampula movie theatre, conveying the memory of a time brimming with future that quickly turned into a 'future of the past'.[35]

---

[30] Cláudia Castelo et al. (eds), *Os outros da colonização: ensaios sobre o colonialismo tardio em Moçambique* (Lisbon: Imprensa das Ciências Sociais, 2012), p. 20.
[31] Caio Simões Araújo, 'Whites, but Not Quite: Settler Imaginations in Late Colonial Mozambique, c. 1951–1964', in *Rethinking White Societies in Southern Africa, 1930s–1990s*, ed. by Duncan Money and Danelle van Zyl-Hermann (London: Routledge, 2020), pp. 97–114.
[32] Castelo, *Os outros da colonização*, p. 23.
[33] José Capão, 'Ilha de Moçambique: sem desenvolvimento não há conservação', *Oceanos*, 25 (1996), 67–74 (p. 68).
[34] Coelho, 'The Enchanted Cloth', p. 15.
[35] Ibid.

The late colonialism evoked by the bridge and by Mr Rashid's memories is also an era defined by 'a repressive developmentalism [...] and processes of engineering of socio-cultural differentiation'.[36] In Mozambique, the 'production of otherness' meant, for the colonial power, taking advantage of the divisions and rivalries that characterized the ethnic-racial and religious groups and communities of the colony. Among these, the Islamic communities presented their own complexities insofar as the conflicts and differentiations stemmed from multiple factors, namely cultural, political, socio-economic, and were also associated with geographical origins. Macagno illustrates how the colonial power first created and dealt with the macro-category of 'Asians', only to shatter it later, by differentiating it on the basis of the imaginary and narratives associated with the danger and threat that the different groups it entailed posed to the regime: Indian-Hindus, Muslims, Chinese, Arab-Muslims.[37] Machaqueiro pinpoints the second half of the 1960s as a moment of change in the colonial political strategy regarding Islamic communities, marked by an orientalist paradigm that opposed an African, syncretic and impure Islam to an Arab-Asian, rigid and pure Islam.[38] To this author, this constitutes a dichotomous and reductive paradigm that, *mutatis mutandis*, also ended up influencing the relations of postcolonial political power with the internal complexities of Muslim communities.

Thus, upon leaving the bridge toward the tailor's shop, that element — once returned, though partially, to its historical and material context — becomes a material and metaphorically significant trace for decoding the temporalities and memories actualized by the narrative. Located on the Island, which in turn acts as a literary bridge between Mozambique and the Indian Ocean,[39] the bridge in the story allows, or not, for the transit between eras, hinting at the complex transition — perhaps the mystery mentioned by the narrator — from late colonialism, when the colonial periphery increasingly separates itself from the metropolitan centre, to postcolonial time, that is, a time in which 'colonial experience appears, simultaneously, to be consigned to the past and, precisely due to the modalities with which its "overcoming" comes about, to be installed at the centre of contemporary social experience'.[40]

---

[36] Miguel Bandeira Jerónimo and António Costa Pinto, 'A Modernizing Empire? Politics, Culture and Economy in Portuguese Late Colonialism', in *The Ends of European Colonial Empires: Cases and Comparisons*, ed. by Miguel Bandeira Jerónimo and António Costa Pinto (Basingstoke: Palgrave Macmillan, 2015), pp. 51–80 (p. 51).

[37] Lorenzo Macagno, 'Árabo-muçulmanos no imaginário luso-tropicalista', in *Os outros da colonização*, ed. by Cláudia Castelo et al. (Lisbon: Imprensa das Ciências Sociais, 2012), pp. 51–70 (pp. 51–52).

[38] Mário Machaqueiro, 'The Islamic Policy of Portuguese Colonial Mozambique, 1960–1973', *The Historical Journal*, 55.4 (2012), 1097–1116 (p. 1100).

[39] Falconi, 'The Lusophone Space', p. 399.

[40] Sandro Mezzadra and Federico Rahola, 'The Postcolonial Condition: A Few Notes on the Quality of Historical Time in the Global Present', in *Reworking Postcolonialism: Globalization, Labour and Rights*, ed. by Pavan Kumar Malreddy et al. (Basingstoke: Palgrave Macmillan, 2015), pp. 36–54 (p. 40).

The enchanted cloth signalled by the title is the material element that becomes central to the narrative. Like the bridge, the cloth also carries connection and relationship by immediately evoking the importance of textiles in the Indian Ocean world, considered the 'historical epicenter of textile innovation and trade'[41] where they actually functioned as elements of economic and cultural integration.[42] Mr Rashid mentions the wide variety of textiles available in colonial times, evoking the integration of the Island in the circuit of distribution and transformation of this product, mostly coming from India, and the socio-economic differentiations of their consumption. Resuming and amplifying the ambivalence of the bridge mentioned at the beginning of the story, the cloth, too, is imbued with duplicity, functioning, at various levels, as an element of connection and separation. In the enchanted cloth, Jamal embroiders secretly from his boss a sophisticated religious cartography, combining different itineraries. The front features the itinerary of his own sacred journey which, from his house in the Macaripe neighbourhood, takes him through the East African coast and the Indian Ocean to Mecca and from there back to the Island, depicting cities, towns and islands of the Islamic, African and Arab geography. On the back, which is where 'one finds the roots, the secret to the enigma that is each piece of embroidery', the young man embroiders a visual narrative of the remote origins of the brotherhood to which he belongs, the Shadhuliyya Madaniyya. It is a story of ramifications, rivalries and conflicts, where the above-mentioned action of the Portuguese colonial power had a part to play and which contributed to shaping the current diversity of Islamic communities in Mozambique.[43]

The materiality of the enchanted cloth summons the materiality of maps: as Farinelli recalls, the link between maps and cloths remains in the etymology of the word 'map', of Punic origin, which referred to a cloth, usually linen, and sometimes embroidered, used to wrap and transport objects, 'each map [being] a movable container'.[44] In the novel *By the Sea* by Zanzibarian writer Abdulrazak Gurnah, Samuelson highlights an analogous connection between cartography and narrative, pointing to 'storytelling as a medium for tracing along the littoral and enabling passage between distant places, rendering the sea a connective tissue rather than divisive element'.[45] In the story, the sea as 'connective tissue' is literally materialized in the cloth, which goes from being a piece of material culture to becoming a map, that is, an artefact of cultural memory that combines connections and fractures, internal and external, at

---

[41] Pedro Machado et al. (eds), *Textile Trades, Consumer Cultures, and the Material Worlds of the Indian Ocean* (Basingstoke: Palgrave Macmillan, 2018), p. 4.

[42] Jeremy Prestholdt, 'The Fabric of the Indian Ocean World: Reflections on the Life Cycle of Cloth', in *Textile Trades, Consumer Cultures, and the Material Worlds of the Indian Ocean*, ed. by Pedro Machado et al. (Basingstoke: Palgrave Macmillan, 2018), pp. 385–96 (p. 387).

[43] Liazzat Bonate, 'Islam in Northern Mozambique: A Historical Overview', *History Compass*, 8.7 (2010), 573–93.

[44] Franco Farinelli, *La crisi della ragione cartografica* (Turin: Einaudi, 2009), p. 38.

[45] Samuelson, 'Narrative Cartographies', p. 79.

local (the Island), national (Mozambique) and transnational (the Islamic Indian Ocean) levels.

Similar to the muddy light that penetrates the old and dark tailor's shop, the focus on the materiality — of the cloth and the map — sheds light on how the religious contrast overlaps with the class struggle, between boss and employee, and at the same time expresses different memories and narratives related to the Indian Ocean. For Mr Rashid, cloths are essentially commodities, links to a colonial and commodified Indian Ocean that is actualized in the transactions engendered by contemporary tourism. His gestures — measuring, tracing, scratching, cutting — are also reminiscent of authoritarian operations of mapping and cartography of cloths/maps and bodies/territories. For Jamal, the cloth is 'a piece of cloth of no importance, boss. Something of mine. To pass the time'.[46] Brown's reflections about objects upon formulating thing theory are relevant in this context insofar as they highlight the special status acquired by objects, which become things when they lose their usual function or are diverted from the 'circuits of production and distribution, consumption and exhibition', drawing attention to their 'thingness', that is, something that expresses the relationship between subject and object.[47] The enchanted cloth leaves the process of commodification and becomes a visual narrative that portrays a religious geography, where one may find an Indian Ocean of the past, conveying a cultural memory — the history of the brotherhood on the back — as well as an Indian Ocean of the future, associated with the individual trajectory — the sacred journey that Jamal has yet to undertake. The religious conflict unfolds and reflects upon the conflict generated by the commodification of the cloth once again imposed by Mr Rashid, leading to the possible tragic outcome foreshadowed in the epilogue.

In addition, given the role and the multiple biographies of textiles in the Indian Ocean world, the small tailor's shop on the Island of Mozambique also stands as a symbol of the declensions in the life of these objects over time and space — from commodities and products of material culture, which also served as elements of integration of the imperial and colonial economies, to increasingly 'enchanted' objects, conveyors of global identities.[48]

As a conclusion to this section focused on the Island of Mozambique, it should be mentioned that Licínio Azevedo's documentary, *A Ilha dos Espíritos* [*The Island of Spirits*], also dedicates some shots to the bridge and the cloths, associating them with the lives and memories of the island's inhabitants. As the title indicates, the documentary focuses on popular beliefs in spirits, building on the dialectic between material/immaterial heritage and between cultural and individual memory, further reflecting on the musealization process begun

---

[46] Coelho, 'The Enchanted Cloth', p. 26.
[47] Brown, 'Thing Theory', p. 4.
[48] Prestholdt, 'The Fabric', p. 395.

in the 1990s with the UNESCO seal of approval.[49] The documentary, too, features the bridge as the inaugural plane of the narrative, in this case framed from the island, associating it with Islam through the focus on the daily life of its guardian, Mamude. The ritual dimension of daily prayers unfolds in the ritualization of the opening and closing of the bar for the entry and exit of vehicles, with the guardian functioning as a link between the Island and the outside.

Cloths also appear as a version of the famous *capulanas*, powerful symbols of East African coastal textile culture and of cultural identities that combine local, national and transnational elements. Framed from the back inside a room, two Makuan women converse, telling of memories evoked by *capulanas* and jewellery, the *capulanas* being an object that 'marks the rhythm of personal history'.[50] It is objects and memories, as opposed to buildings and palaces, that join the memories and legends of the spirits, constituting a material and immaterial secondary heritage that remains on the fringes of the official narratives.

In both narratives, the historical and cultural connection between the Island and the Indian Ocean emerges from fragments, objects and traces, which are in turn associated with identitarian narratives and memories, both individual and collective, that project the Indian Ocean as a cultural space, as defined by Vergès and Marimoutou:

> It is a cultural space overarched by several chronotopes, where temporalities and territorialities are constructed and deconstructed. An ocean linking continents and islands. A space that is Afro-Asiatic, Moslem, Christian, Animist, Buddhist, Hindu, and creolised. An ocean of trade winds, monsoons, cyclones and winds. [...] It is piecemeal and fragmented, but also traversed by common itineraries; this ocean is marked by the different temporalities found there: Malayo-Indonesian, globalisation, the Muslim economic world, European thalassocracy, pre-European global empires, trade and slavery, and European empires.[51]

Of Gifts and Debts, on Timor Island

Despite the slow and methodical construction of its historical and conceptual unity, the Indian Ocean as described remains a fluid universe and system, open to other connections and crossed by multiple circulations that, over time,

---

[49] Ana Mafalda Leite and Jessica Falconi, 'Island of Mozambique: Narratives from a Contact Zone', in *Cities of the Lusophone World*, ed. by Doris Wieser and Filipa Prata (Oxford: Peter Lang, 2018), pp. 69–92.

[50] Maria Paula Meneses, 'As capulanas de Moçambique: descodificando mensagens, procurando sentidos nos tecidos', in *Método, métodos, contramétodo*, ed. by Regina Leite Garcia (São Paulo: Cortez Editora, 2003), pp. 111–23 (p. 116).

[51] Françoise Vergès and Carpanin Marimoutou, 'Moorings: Indian Ocean Creolizations', *Portal: Journal of Multidisciplinary International Studies*, 9.1 (2012), 1–39 (p. 14).

have shaped its imaginaries and representations. The focus on circulation and on the 'multi-cornered' nature of maritime networks emerges as an innovative approach in maritime and oceanic studies, as it allows us to view the movement of people, ideas and goods as an essentially multidirectional movement that breaks with the metropolis/colonies binarity.[52] However, the inclusion of a narrative centred on East Timor in the itinerary herein proposed merits a brief clarification concerning the definition of the limits and boundaries of oceans in general and of the Indian Ocean in particular. This is a complex issue, from which only a few aspects discussed in maritime historiography should be retained. If the inclusion of the East African coast in the history of the Indian Ocean is now consensual, the boundaries to the east and southeast have raised questions related to the formulation of the concept of maritime space and its material and immaterial fluidity. As argued by Ray, maritime space is not defined solely in geographical and environmental terms; rather, it is 'the product of complex interaction between communities and the physical factors'.[53] While seeking to define the Indian Ocean as a maritime space and historical unit, Pearson recognizes that 'The eastern boundaries of the ocean are porous, with the Indian Ocean flowing imperceptibly into the South China Sea and the Pacific Ocean' and points to the Strait of Malacca and northwestern Australia as possible boundaries, further claiming that the combined economy of southern Asia 'dwarfs all the others around the ocean's rim'.[54] Alpers, too, dwells upon this matter, stating that

> The simple answer is that it encompasses everything from the Cape of Good Hope into the Red Sea, across to the South China Sea, and down to Australia, but as one begins to think about the Indian Ocean as a historical region it is useful to keep in mind that both the reality and the idea of the Indian Ocean have changed over time.[55]

Reid underlines the scant attention paid to Southeast Asia in the field of Indian Ocean Studies, pointing to the importance of inquiring into the connections and exchanges that have shaped the cultures of this area.[56] Building on this assumption, Engelenhoven and Krakowska propose a collection of fragments and traces of the cultural transits between Timor and the Indian Ocean based on the analysis of oral narratives.[57]

---

[52] Himanshu Prabha Ray, 'Crossing the Seas: Connecting Maritime Spaces in Colonial India', in *Cross Currents and Community Networks: The History of the Indian Ocean Worlds*, ed. by Himanshu Prabha Ray and Edward Alpers (New Delhi: Oxford University Press, 2007), pp. 50–77 (p. 51).
[53] Ray, 'Crossing the Seas', p. 50.
[54] Pearson, *The Indian Ocean*, p. 10.
[55] Alpers, *The Indian Ocean in World History*, p. 6.
[56] Anthony Reid, 'Aceh between Two Worlds: An Intersection of Southeast Asia and the Indian Ocean', in *Cross Currents and Community Networks: The History of the Indian Ocean World*, ed. by Himanshu P. Ray and Edward Alpers (New Delhi: Oxford University Press, 2007), pp. 100–32 (p. 100).
[57] Aone van Engelenhoven and Kamila Krakowska Rodrigues, 'O Sudeste Asiático e o Oceano Índico: reflexões sobre trânsitos linguísticos e travessias culturais nas tradições orais em Timor-Leste', *Remate de Males*, 38.1 (2018), 220–39.

In light of these considerations, and taking into account the characterization of the Indian Ocean 'as a coherent, if multicentered historical unit whose ports were connected by oceanic travel',[58] LC's novel *Requiem for the Solitary Sailor* is summoned here because it projects the connection of Timor to the Indian Ocean in a peripheral way, associated with the transit and circulation of people and things between the ports of the Indian and Pacific Oceans and the former Portuguese imperial space, where the island, historically and geographically, acts as a hinge between worlds, times and seas. As in JPBC's short story, through material culture and materiality, the characters in the novel project and negotiate notions of identity and belonging that transcend strictly territorial boundaries, functioning as characters whose cultural 'origin' is essentially 'oceanic', that is, built by the circulation of ideas, people and objects in the Indian Ocean. The novel, like a 'logbook' of the protagonist's solitary journey through the vicissitudes of personal and collective history, focuses on Timor at the time of the Second World War and the Japanese invasion. Daniel Silva, whose analysis of this novel will be referred to several times, points to mobility in LC's writing as 'a trope of trans-spatial movement' that positions narrators and characters 'in flux through spaces and positions of power, privilege and capital'.[59] Thus, literal, literary and metaphorical navigations and crossings, already evoked in the title alluding to Alain Gerbault, project this movement and mark the trajectories of the characters, the first of whom is the protagonist/narrator, who docks in Timor aboard a Dutch freighter 'on the line where the land ends and the sea begins, and at the moment when the Sea-Man blends with the Sea-Woman'.[60]

The peculiar positioning of the island of Timor among economic and cultural maritime systems, its connection to the Indian Ocean, and the centrality of circulation between the multiple imperial peripheries, appear as traces when we pay attention to the diverse origins of the characters that gravitate around the port of Dili. Catarina witnesses the formation of Chinese communities in Indonesia, being the daughter of a Chinese merchant from Batavia, whose trajectory, first associated with the course of the Yellow River, is described as wandering from port to port in search of good business and prosperity. The origins of other characters are also indicative of intra- and inter-imperial connections that render the Timorese space 'first and foremost as a dizzying conjunction of imperial actors and forces'.[61] The Dili port captains and other figures represent what Gupta defines as 'the uniquely itinerant quality of Portuguese colonialism',[62] pointing to the mobility of people in the

---

[58] Alpers, *The Indian Ocean in World History*, p. 6.
[59] Daniel Silva, *Anti-Empire: Decolonial Interventions in Lusophone Literatures* (Liverpool: Liverpool University Press, 2018), pp. 145–46.
[60] Luís Cardoso, *Requiem para o navegador solitário* (Lisbon: Dom Quixote, 2007), p. 179.
[61] Silva, *Anti-Empire*, p. 150.
[62] Pamila Gupta, *Portuguese Decolonization in the Indian Ocean World* (London: Bloomsbury Academic, 2017), p. 11.

Portuguese imperial space as a systemic phenomenon. This is the case with Alberto Sacramento Monteiro, captain of the port of Dili, born in Goa to a Portuguese father and a Goan mother, owner of a coffee plantation in Timor; and César Semedo, another captain, hailing from Cape Verde. Other traces of circulation in the Indian Ocean emerge when we look at the figure of Indian Jones, an adventurer from Ceylon and provider of various services, as well as Sir Lawrence, a merchant from Bengal also engaged in several activities. Together with Sacramento, the three constitute the so-called 'Trinity of the Malabar Coast', who usually meet at the emblematic Salazar Hotel, a key location of cosmopolitan appearance in the colonial port city:

> They spoke Portuguese, Tetum, Bengali, Malay, and once in a while you could hear a whole sentence in English — How we alone of mortals are — Such confusion of languages seemed to be a small sample of what a babel would be. Or perhaps a brothel, like dark dens of the ports in a great metropolis where sailors from several continents cross paths.[63]

In this novel, materiality is elicited by specific elements and objects and also emerges as a systemic dimension that regulates human relations and participates in the construction of identities. As already demonstrated,[64] LC's fiction establishes an explicit relationship with the history of East Timor, which in *Requiem* is symbolized by the political-military conflicts that ravage the island, intertwined with the economic exploitation of the territory and of indigenous labour. The deals for the exploitation of resources and the distribution of products — coffee, cotton, salt — constitute a layer of materiality that motivates relationships and alliances between the characters, openly pointing to a network of interests and conflicts that bind both the island and Catarina. The logic and rituals of commercial transactions, as well as the consumption, use and exchange of objects, mark Catarina's memories of the event that lies at the origin of her going to Timor, hence of the narrative. Her union with Sacramento Monteiro, which will not become an official marriage, is in fact the result of a 'marriage' between men, one that seeks to join the commercial activities of her own father and those of the port captain, for the purposes of the import-export of Chinese silk in Timor and Timorese coffee in Batavia. The business marriage will sink, giving rise to Monteiro's debt, which Catarina will have to collect by traveling to Timor. Prior to this, the business conversations over cups of tea, glasses of brandy and opium associate the commodities — coffee from Timor, Chinese silk, tobacco from Java — with seduction and the female body. Catarina captures the systemic nature of the complicities between trade, imperialism and patriarchy through these and other allusions. Take, for instance, the negotiations between her father and Monteiro, during which the presence of a jade cat triggers an ambiguous identification, operated by the male

[63] Cardoso, *Requiem*, p. 21.
[64] Isabel Moutinho, 'Historicity and Storytelling in East Timorese Fiction in Portuguese', *Ellipsis*, 10 (2012), 101–22 (p. 106).

double gaze, between the object and Catarina, transforming the woman into a gift attached to the trade pact:

> The visitor, during the entire time he was in our house, did not take his eyes off either me or a jade item, which represented a cat. Probably his interest in the object served as a cover for another yellow item that was not made of stone, but of flesh and blood and represented a Chinese girl with exotic cultural pretensions. None of this went unnoticed by the old Chinese man who asked if he was interested in the item. With his eyes fixed on me, he said that his curiosity went beyond the symbolic representation of that animal. [...] Before leaving, looking in my direction, he asked for the name of the item, which my father said was called Catarina.
> — Catarina?!
> replied the surprised visitor.[65]

From this misunderstanding, illustrative of Catarina's positioning 'within the masculine sphere of power',[66] the jade cat appears as another enchanted and charming object, of uncertain origin, which is in many ways associated with the identity of the protagonist, materializing fluctuating boundaries between subject and object. According to the account, the item would have appeared at the Batavia house on the day of Catarina's birth, but the circumstances of its appearance are shrouded in doubt: was it won in a bet from an antiques dealer or obtained in exchange for pearls to fascinate visitors? Catarina's other allusions to her family's ties to pirates, smugglers and bandits point to the multiple ways, between the licit and the illicit, of obtaining, exchanging and possessing objects.

A cultural artefact of immemorial origin, which evokes the circulation of cultural objects and traditions at global level, the item is comparable to the 'marginal object' — the antique — described by Baudrillard as being associated with the myth of origins, the event of birth, and the 'family portrait'.[67] It further represents a mythical time that adds to the temporal complexity of the narrative, going 'against Western historicity'.[68] Although different in nature and characteristics from JPBC's enchanted cloth, the jade cat in this novel works in a similar way in terms of materializing a complex notion of cultural identity and belonging that is defined by the wanderings and circulations of the oceans and shaped by both individual and systemic dimensions.

Following the journeys through spaces and times of the characters, the item reappears in Timor, at the house where Catarina lives with her son, the fruit of Monteiro's rape, and with Madalena, another victim of the port captain who also bore him a daughter, Esmeralda. With the women and children also live the cats, other ambiguous gifts that turn into debts: according to the island custom,

---

[65] Cardoso, *Requiem*, p. 15.
[66] Silva, *Anti-Empire*, p. 158.
[67] Jean Baudrillard, 'Subjective Discourse or the Non-Functional System of Objects', in *The Object Reader*, ed. by Fiona Candlin and Raiford Guins (London: Routledge, 2009), pp. 40–64 (p. 42).
[68] Silva, *Anti-Empire*, p. 151.

the offered cats determine Catarina's status as *nona*, a concubine that the port captains pass on as inheritance. Her brother, Lúcius, returns the item to her, informing her of her father's death and promising revenge against Monteiro. At the Timor house Esmeralda promotes the integration of the jade cat into the group of flesh-and-blood cats, and so the place of colonial and patriarchal violence — the Pousada Buganvília — is resignified by Catarina as a place of hospitality and becomes home to a new family, a socio-affective formation that is a human/nonhuman, animate/inanimate set, capable of projecting another possible form of subordinate alliance, not founded on or regulated by the logics of power and commercial transactions.

In its journey throughout the narrative, the item exerts a fascination on Alain Gerbault, who wonders about its origins, possibly wanting to wonder about Catarina's past. Indian Jones projects his desires onto the item, christening it 'Catarina, the other', a name that is also repeated by the 'real' Catarina. The fascination of the item and the fluctuating relationship Catarina establishes with it reveal the object's ambiguous power to objectify her — a silk doll, a stranded boat — and at the same time make her a subject by declaring the 'otherness' of the item. We can see in this power what Brown defines as the *thingness* of objects, 'their force as a sensuous presence or as a metaphysical presence, the magic by which objects become values, fetishes, idols, and totems'.[69] Also characterized by a status that oscillates between that of a gift, remembrance of debt, and inheritance, like Catarina herself in the 'plot' created by others, the item points to 'ambiguous possessions'[70] and identifications that blur the distinctions between subjects and objects, between what/who possesses and what/who is possessed. It alludes to Catarina's position in the network of male desires and powers, and to Timor's place in the network of intra- and inter-imperial relationships and conflicts highlighted by the narrative. This ambiguity extends to the possession and ownership of Fazenda Sacromonte, the coffee plantation, confiscated from the rebels of Manumera and donated to Monteiro, inherited by Catarina as payment of his debt, and again shared with the indigenous Malisera, in a chain of alliances and betrayals that entangle the relations of authority and power in the colonial and capitalist world-system.

On the eve of the Japanese invasion of the island, the jade cat disappears and a fire destroys Catarina's Timorese home and her human/nonhuman family. Only one object reappears, by the hand of Sir Lawrence: the kerosene lamp, signalling the wait and the memory that illuminates the future of a possible reunion of Catarina with her kidnapped son.

As highlighted by other studies, the movement across spaces and times also happens between novels, where characters and, one might add, objects transition from one story to the next. In *O ano em que Pigafetta completou a circum-navegação* [*The Year Pigafetta Completed the Circumnavigation*] (2013),

---

[69] Brown, *Thing Theory*, p. 5.
[70] Samuelson, 'Narrative Cartographies', p. 81.

centred on another appropriation/modernization of the journey imaginary, this time to fictionalize the recent history of East Timor, both the kerosene lamp and the characters of Catarina and Malisera reappear, bringing fragments of their stories and encounters. However, what stands out at the very incipit of this novel is the fact that the left sandal of a pair of leather sandals, acquired by Amadeu as a gift to his daughter Carolina, is the inaugural narrating voice that, together with the right twin, follows the whole narrative and the identity journey of its protagonist — yet another 'enchanted thing' whose duplicity provides a powerful material metaphor and literary device for narrating from two oceans.

Conclusions

Among the many differences that mark the two texts analysed in this article, the most evident common elements are the insular location and the presence of enchanted things that actively participate in the construction of memories and identities: on one hand, the Island of Mozambique, its bridge that connects and separates worlds and epochs, and its enchanted cloths that connect and separate individuals, memories and ideas of the Indian Ocean; and on the other, the Island of Timor, itself a bridge between two oceans, the destination of multiple journeys, like that of a jade cat of uncertain provenance and unknown fate. In slightly different ways, though they can be traced back to similar issues, both narratives suggest, more or less explicitly, the idea that not everything that can be seen on the islands is revealed in their meanings.

In the final part of JPBC's short story, this idea is suggested by the very making of the enchanted cloth: faced with Jamal's cloth, perceived as 'a strange piece of coarse cloth of uncertain color', the 'we' with which the narrator identifies on occasion claims he does not see in the embroidery — either back or front, — 'any more than the Island',[71] unable to distinguish between the drawing of the Island and that of sacred history, that is, unable to grasp the charm of the cloth.

In LC's novel, this idea is explicitly formulated by the narrator at the beginning of the narrative, which evolves through flashbacks:

> Now that I am climbing up shortcuts that lead me back to Mount Manumera, I realize that the island where I made an appointment with my prince charming has gems that only the curious gaze of interested people can bring to the light of day.
>
> Not everything that can be seen is uncovered. The mist and the shadow still hover over the stones that adorn the mountaintops.[72]

In both cases, mention is made of the islands — as drawing in JPBC, as landscape in LC — and of the act of seeing — to distinguish and to uncover,

---

[71] Coelho, 'The Enchanted Cloth', p. 34.
[72] Cardoso, *Requiem*, p. 11.

respectively. In both cases, there is a call for materialities, surfaces, visibilities, and the (in)ability to decipher embroidery and stones. In both cases, what is seen, the mute materiality — without voice — does not account for the whole story(ies), inviting us to distinguish and discover them. It is necessary, perhaps, to make things speak and tell stories, which is what we have sought to do in this article, albeit partially, in order to shed light on memories and identities of islands and oceans.

East Timorese Literary Narratives (Twenty-First Century): Indian Ocean Crossings and Littoral Encounters

Giulia Spinuzza

CEsA — Center for African and Development Studies,
ISEG, University of Lisbon

Based on the analysis of the book *Requiem para o navegador solitário* [*Requiem for the Solitary Sailor*] published in 2007 by Timorese writer Luís Cardoso,[1] we aim to investigate further the author's literary strategies in the process of construction of the female protagonist, focusing specifically on the maritime elements related to the coastal geography (such as the port, the sea, the boats, the balcony, among others). In fact, we believe that these elements integrate not only the geographical space of the narrative, but also the author's literary imaginary, as is the case, for example, of the metaphorical resources and the construction of the main character, Catarina. Considering that East Timor is located on the eastern rim of the Indian Ocean and taking into account the theoretical framework of Indian Ocean Studies, we aim to demonstrate that in this novel the ocean constitutes a visual and metaphorical transcontinental repertoire that engages with the very Timorese cultural imaginary.

Since his first book, *Crónica de uma travessia: a época do Ai-Dik-Funam* (1997), the writer Luís Cardoso has narrated the biographical, maritime or metaphorical crossings of the main characters. It is based on this perspective of texts *in itinere* that we frame the author's work in the broader concept of Indian Ocean, considering that it marks the author's worldview and his narrative strategies.

Based on a critical reading of the novel, we intend to highlight the interweaving of multiple crossings on Timorese territory. Navigations are undoubtedly the hallmark of the Portuguese language narrative, either in a utopian and celebratory vision, or in its dystopian reverse. We are interested in studying these aspects especially after the collapse of the colonial empire, which

---

[1] Luís Cardoso, a writer of the Timorese diaspora, is one of the most striking literary voices in contemporary Timorese literature. His first work, published in 1997, was *Crónica de uma travessia* (translated into English under the title *The Crossing: The Story of East Timor*). In 2013 he published *O ano em que Pigafetta completou a circum-navegação* and his most recent book was *O plantador de abóboras* (2020).

allows us to identify a process of rewriting and questioning of the imaginary associated with ocean crossings within the then Portuguese empire. Consider, for instance, the work of Mia Couto, *O Outro Pé da Sereia*, among others.

In *Requiem for the Solitary Sailor*, the imaginary connected to the navigations is transposed to the idea of existential crossing. In this sense, we aim to combine the reflection on the crossing-related imaginary with the identification of a coastal and insular maritime imaginary. In fact, the sea is not only the backdrop to this narrative, but it is one of the recurring visual elements of Cardoso's writing, in metaphorical and metonymic terms, as well as in material terms, owing to the constant presence of maritime and coastal elements, notably the port that conveys the arrival of new protagonists (the port captains, the solitary sailor, the occupation troops, among others). Thus, we can say that Dili evinces a certain coastal porosity,[2] which makes this space the stage of intersections of the various characters that populate the novel. The port, in particular, acts as a kaleidoscope that fragments worldviews and absorbs different cultures and identities that cross paths in this place; it is a porous space, as is the very insular territory of Timor.

In *Cultures of Trades: Indian Ocean Exchanges*, Devleena Ghosh and Stephen Muecke highlight the unity and, at the same time, the fragmentary character of the liminal spaces of the Indian Ocean, claiming that the 'Indian Ocean is a kind of Foucauldian heterotopia, a space of diverse, fragmentary and alternative narratives which empirically resist any formalising gaze'.[3]

Considering Ghosh and Muecke's observations, we believe we may combine our analysis with some of the remarks by Daniel F. Silva, according to whom Cardoso's works also offer, at a narrative level, a historicization that promotes alternative 'narratives of Empire'.[4] Silva's study highlights issues of gender and power in the colonial context, bearing in mind the peculiar historical moment in which the novel takes place, that is, during the Second World War, a period in which Timor experienced successive occupations, in the face of Portugal's apparent neutrality. In fact, the country was occupied first by Australian and Dutch troops and then by the Japanese empire. As we will see, the violence and oppression endured by Catarina, the protagonist and narrator, can be interpreted in the light of the dramatic and violent history of the country.

The beginning of the story takes us to the early 1940s in Batavia,[5] from where Catarina leaves for Timor in search of her fiancé, the captain of the

---

[2] Meg Samuelson, 'Coastal Form: Amphibian Positions, Wider Worlds, and Planetary Horizons on the African Indian Ocean Littoral', *Comparative Literature*, 69.1 (2017), 16–24 (p. 22), <https://doi.org/10.1215/00104124-3794569>.
[3] Devleena Ghosh and Stephen Muecke (eds), *Cultures of Trade: Indian Ocean Exchanges* (Newcastle upon Tyne: Cambridge Scholars, 2007), p. 5.
[4] Daniel F. Silva, 'Untranslatable Subalternity and Historicizing Empire's Enjoyment in Luís Cardoso's *Requiem para o Navegador Solitário*', in *Anti-Empire: Decolonial Interventions in Lusophone Literatures* (Liverpool: Liverpool University Press, 2018), Chapter 4, pp. 145–72 (p. 148), <https://doi.org/10.2307/j.ctv69tgxz>.
[5] Batavia was formerly a Dutch colony that was part of present-day Jakarta, Indonesia.

port of Dili (now the country's capital) and a business associate of the young woman's father. Catarina is the fruit of the union between several orients: her father is 'a Chinese man from the continent who went down along the Yellow River' and her mother a 'beautiful woman, fruit of a relationship between a Creole woman and a colonial governor'.[6] The parents, itinerant subjects along the oriental coasts, 'went from town to town in search of a safe port' (p. 13). An interest in developing a coffee planting business caused her father to come in contact with the Dili port captain. The action of the novel is then triggered by the protagonist's fiancé, Alberto Sacramento Monteiro, born in Goa to a Portuguese father and now captain of the port of Dili.

This city is described by Catarina at the very beginning of the novel as 'a land full of swamps and crocodiles, infested with mosquitoes and malaria, to which the Portuguese sent their officials fallen in disgrace, with the task of caring for other countrymen, even more disgraced, sent there in exile' (p. 14). This first sad image contrasts with the vision of the beautiful bay of Dili that the protagonist mentions later, but it is interesting to note that this brief description refers to some aspects linked to the insalubrity of the land and also suggests a problematic colonial interaction between the former metropolis and Timor, one of the most distant colonies of the empire. This matter relates to the fact that the port captain is of Goan origin, another former Portuguese colony, which points to the relations between the spaces of the then Lusitanian empire, evoking at the same time a location that falls within the context of the Indian Ocean geography.

The beginning of the novel is marked by the network of trade and commercial interests of the eastern ports. As soon as the narrative moves to Timor, the port of Dili becomes another protagonist of this story. Inhabited by prostitutes, convicts, sailors and cats, the port is the place of comings and goings that characterize the narrative of the novel. It then becomes a significant element of this text, contributing to the development of the maritime imaginary.

The Timorese geographical imaginary emerges clearly when the protagonist decides to explore the bay of Dili and becomes fascinated by the view of the sea that marks the geography of the city. It is during one of the first strolls that the narrator describes the coastal and insular landscape:

> The following morning, I went on an excursion to get to know the city and its beautiful bay. [...] I stopped by the jetty to take a look at the horizon, with Ataúro Island hovering in the distance. Also sights of other smaller islands [...]. I was especially charmed by one of them for it was named Lira. The desire to someday retire to that place pervaded me. (pp. 20–21)

However, the idyllic image of the bay is interrupted by the violence that marks Catarina's arrival in Dili. Indeed, shortly after arriving in Timor to inquire

---

[6] Luís Cardoso, *Requiem para o navegador solitário* (Lisbon: Dom Quixote, 2007), p. 13 (translations from this novel and other Portuguese sources are my own). Henceforth page numbers will be shown in the text.

about the family business, Catarina, object of trade between her father and her fiancé, is raped by the captain. In order to describe such a violent act, the narrator resorts to elements of the maritime world: 'he thrust himself on me like a sea wolf' (p. 35). Shortly after the dramatic experience of rape by her fiancé, Catarina seeks peace in the waters of the sea: 'I plunged into the waves to save myself. At the time it didn't even occur to me to think about the consequences of my act. It was the sea that awaited me with open arms' (p. 36). If the two moments are marked by the maritime world, we can also see that this violent act was somehow pre-announced upon arriving at the port of Dili, as we can read in the following excerpt: 'I arrived in the city of Dili aboard a Dutch freighter, under a fiery dusk sky, a mixture of colours between yellow and red which seemed to me to announce a biblical catastrophe' (p. 18). In sum, all three moments (pre-announcement, act, and epiphany in the sea waters) of the violence to which the protagonist is subjected are defined by the imaginary of the maritime world.

Another striking aspect of this novel is the geographical space inhabited by Catarina. One of the central places of this novel is the villa of Pousada Buganvília with its wide balcony overlooking the sea: 'Sometimes it is harder to navigate on land than on sea. The only difference is that those who arrive from the sea always have someone waiting for them on a balcony carpeted with bougainvilleas' (p. 154). As the story unfolds, Catarina will acquire the habit of spending her time sitting in that space contemplating the sea while reading the book she took with her from Batavia, *À la poursuite du soleil*, by the French navigator Alain Gerbault, who died in Dili in 1941 and who had completed his single-handed circumnavigation of the earth approximately a decade earlier. It is on the balcony that the narrator awaits the sailor's arrival, while enjoying a serene contemplation of the sea:

> I would often stand there on the balcony looking at the sea, at the horizon line or at the nothingness. Perhaps in search of something to which I could direct my attention, a seagull, a sailboat or simply nothing. Absolutely nothing but the sea, a huge expanse of smooth water without a flaw or a wrinkle to hold my attention. I wandered beyond the line that separates the sea from the sky and into a desert of white clouds. Everything looked the same as it always had. (p. 85)

The balcony is the point of contact between reality and dream/hope, whereas the Sea of Arafura dematerializes and conveys the moment when the intimacy of the poetic subject meets with infinity. The sea represents tranquillity and triggers the reverie of the protagonist, who loses herself in the maritime horizon line. To better understand this facet of the sea as a contemplative element, we refer to the studies of Bachelard, who deems the images elicited by the aquatic element ontological in nature. As remarked by the French philosopher, the being is reflected in the images of immensity provided by the maritime and celestial horizon. Water also represents a destination, 'no longer merely the destination of fleeting images, the vain destination of a dream that does not end, but an essential destination that incessantly metamorphoses the substance of being'.[7]

Furthermore, if we focus more specifically on the narrator's vision from the coast, we can argue that the balcony of the Pousada Buganvília offers an amphibious aesthetic vision, as Meg Samuelson defines it. This critic, who develops in literary studies Michael N. Pearson's call for amphibious stories,[8] states that the coast can provide an amphibious vision, which conveys a bifocal perspective sometimes targeting the land, sometimes the sea. Thus, the narrator's ontological reflection with her gaze fixed upon the maritime horizon embodies a series of maritime images that move across land and sea, as can be seen in the continuation of the excerpt quoted above: 'Madalena needed to put her arm around my waist to pull me out of that place. As if I were a sailboat stranded on a coral bank' (p. 86). This ontological condition of the subject, constantly equated with maritime elements but with feet firmly set on land, seems to us to express the concept of amphibian aesthetics elaborated by Samuelson.

From the balcony, Catarina waits not only for the solitary sailor, but also for her father, 'the old Chinese man' coming from the sea to rescue her (p. 86), just as from the port of Dili some of the locals were waiting for the arrival of the Portuguese ship amid the Second World War (pp. 152, 180). But neither Catarina's father nor the Portuguese ship arrives in Dili.

As for the solitary sailor, Catarina knows that 'it is madness to wait for an adventurer. He would never seek shelter on an island like Timor, which, although known as a land where the sun rose, was rather the place where they sent those poor people that others rejected' (p. 86). This excerpt resumes the idea of Timor as a land of convicts, as demonstrated by Teresa Cunha: 'Timor in general and Dili in particular were transfigured into a non-place, because it was the destination of deportees, exiles and the *incorrigibles* from India, Macau, Mozambique and Portugal, because it was so far away and had such inclement weather that it was the concrete and material land of oblivion and isolation'.[9] Thus, Timor appears as an island that gives shelter to those who, like the protagonist, were rejected, not so much for political reasons like most exiles, but as a wife and a woman.

Although the sea around the island remains in a sense a prison for Catarina, it also represents an opening. Indeed, the woman longs for maritime spaces to escape her tragic fate, because not even the mountains of the interior, where the Timorese took refuge in their resistance against the occupations, are a safe place for the narrator. Taking into account the dramatic history of the country,

---

[7] Gaston Bachelard, *A água e os sonhos: ensaio sobre a imaginação da matéria* [1942], trans. by António de Pádua Danesi (São Paulo: Martins Fontes, 1989), pp. 6–7.
[8] Samuelson, p. 20.
[9] Teresa Cunha, 'Para além de um índico de desespero e revoltas' (unpublished doctoral dissertation, Universidade de Coimbra, 2010), p. 33, <http://hdl.handle.net/10316/15382>.

we can argue that Catarina becomes, in a way, a metonymy of the violated country, evoking a possible country/woman binomial, which is also found in autobiographical texts such as Fátima Guterres's *Timor: Paraíso Violentado* [Timor: Violated Paradise] (2014).

But if on the one hand the woman can be interpreted metaphorically as a violated country, on the other hand, in Cardoso's novel, it is the country itself that becomes the rapist. In fact, in the protagonist's reflection about the dramatic event that marks her arrival in Timor, the narrator resorts once again to the maritime metaphor and identifies the torturer with the imagery of the crocodile:

> At the moment when I needed my mother's comfort, I was alone and left to myself. Worse than all this, I was thrown into the crocodile's mouth by my own father. I was like a damaged ship in the waters of a hostile country, thinking of his status as port captain, which should in principle offer me shelter. (p. 39)

The crocodile is the protagonist of the founding myth of the Timorese territory and a central element in the Timorese cultural imaginary, because, according to legend, after a long journey it turned into the island of Timor. In addition to metaphorically evoking Catarina's crossing to the mouth of the crocodile/Sacramento Monteiro, identified with the Timorese country itself, this reflection also evinces a clear oppression of the protagonist by the patriarchal system.

However, despite the identification of the torturer with Timor, we can draw a parallel between the woman and the Timorese country if we think of Catarina's existential path and the history of Timor. In fact, like Catarina, who as the object of desire of the Dili port captains is subjected to different oppressive forces, Timor is also trapped between regional powers and is at the same time the target of imperial aspirations.[10] As Teresa Cunha writes, Timor is geographically located 'at the end of the maritime coast that connects the Indian Ocean to the Australian continent as if it were the last piece of an immense wall that seems to divide worlds and oceans'.[11]

This means that — considering the development of the narrative of the novel, as well as the historical context of the Second World War, the arrival of the Australian and Dutch troops and the ensuing Japanese occupation — Timor is trapped, like the protagonist Catarina, at a historical and geographical crossroads marked by Portuguese colonialism and by the actors of the Second World War (let us not forget that at the time the western part of the Timorese island was a Dutch colony).

As regards the oppressive forces of the protagonist and before we look at some aspects of Silva's study, which investigates this matter in depth, let us remember that Robert Young explains that the double colonization of women

---

[10] Cunha, p. 33.
[11] Cunha, p. 14.

is due to their condition,[12] firstly, in the domestic sphere — 'the patriarchy of men — and, secondly, in the public sphere — the 'patriarchy of the colonial power'.[13] The gender oppression connected to the patriarchal system (Catarina, sold by her father, is raped by her fiancé) and to the colonial oppression (first Portuguese and then Japanese between 1942 and 1946) defines Catarina's condition.

In fact, Catarina is the object of multiple oppression and subjugation processes, as Silva's detailed study has shown. However, as a narrator, it is her vision as a woman that calls into question the 'imperial narratives of masculine and European superiority'.[14] As observed by Silva, Catarina, 'as a woman of Chinese and Indonesian descent, is often the object of different male gazes, as well as the imperial masculine gaze residing behind Empire's epistemological function'.[15] Silva associates this aspect with a gender-related orientalist perspective, whereby in the eyes of the port captain Catarina embodies 'an imperial fantasy of gendered oriental otherness'.[16] It is interesting to note, in this regard, that the person responsible for unmasking this orientalizing narrative is Catarina herself, who with subtle irony describes the look of others upon her own oriental body, with its seductive and magical fascination — 'the sweet charm of the East',[17] as she describes it in an act of sheer deconstruction.

Thus, we can argue that the narrative perspective from the point of view of the female protagonist unveils not only the colonial contradictions and contrasts, but also the gender issues which, especially in the colonial context, engender double (or multiple) oppression of women, as explained above. Indeed, Silva's proposal demonstrates this possibility for the narrative to present a 'de-masculinized/decolonial act of historicization'.[18] If, on the one hand, Catarina becomes a metaphor of the violated land, hence being subjected like Timor to the different imperial powers and to the wills of subjects that do not fit in the sphere of those powers,[19] on the other hand, she accomplishes a performative act, as a narrator (and writer, since in the end she will write the logbook).

Regarding the importance of the logbook, it should be noted that Catarina is the one who writes it at the end of the novel. The protagonist manages to escape the oppression exercised by the patriarchal, masculine and imperial sphere of power, taking shelter in the boat that belonged to the deceased sailor. Thus, the water represents a neutral space, a lifebuoy, a refuge, if partially utopian,

---

[12] Young quotes from the study by Kirsten Holst Petersen and Anna Rutherford, *A Double Colonization: Colonial and Post-Colonial Women's Writing* (Oxford: Dangaroo Press, 1985).
[13] Robert J. C. Young, *Colonial Desire: Hybridity in Theory, Culture and Race* (London: Routledge, 1995), p. 162.
[14] Silva, 'Untranslatable Subalternity', p. 152.
[15] Ibid.
[16] Silva, p. 159.
[17] Silva, p. 112.
[18] Silva, p. 152.
[19] Ibid.

against the violence of the present. Only after having recorded everything in the logbook can she definitively return to the land that welcomed her.

In his study, Silva also underscores the diasporic aspect of the characters in Cardoso's novels: 'what Catarina thus finds in East Timor is arguably more than the intersecting of exilic identities, but also that of global narratives, both imperial and decolonial, in contact and flux'.[20] The critic stresses that 'Cardoso's central characters and narrators are, like him, in flux through spaces and positions of power, privilege, and capital'.[21]

Returning to the matter of diaspora and the idea of flux, we contend that these elements may be associated with the crossing, as well as the fluidity of the identity of the main character in the novel. That is why the maritime metaphors bring the protagonist closer to the elements attached to insular and coastal societies: the port, the boat, the balcony, among others. In fact, the whole narrative of the novel can be read on the margin between the coast and the sea, due not only to the geographic location, marked by insular conformation, but also to the narrative resources.

Thus, we can re-interpret Catarina's existence in the light of an insular imaginary that evokes the geographical dimension of Timor, at a chaotic and violent historical crossroads, sometimes counterposed to the peace of the sea. In fact, the sea appears as a counterpoint imaginary against the violence of the land (although it is through the Indian Ocean that Portuguese colonial power is established).[22] In this sense, we might claim that the sea, on the one hand, bears a historical dimension and, on the other hand, bears an oneiric and utopian dimension, because the waters constitute the repository of dreams. Indeed, as we have seen, the sea sometimes serves as an element of comparison of the human condition and is the repository of dreams, of peace, and of hope, marked by Catarina's wait for the solitary sailor.

Catarina, the *nona*[23] of Batavia, who awaits the arrival of the sailor from the balcony of her own house, inhabits a geographical space set between land and sea. In this regard, we can compare the bougainvillea balcony of Catarina's house with the one forged by some Mozambican poets and writers such as Eduardo White, Mia Couto and João Paulo Borges Coelho, among others, who develop in their works the imaginary of a balcony/city/country overlooking the ocean. This element allows us to rethink the 'nation as coastal form',[24] not only

---

[20] Silva, p. 151.
[21] Silva, p. 146.
[22] Consider the reference to the arrival of the Portuguese boat which was to re-establish Portuguese power on Timorese territory after the beginning of the Second World War or the reference to the *landins* from Mozambique sent to establish the Portuguese colonial order in the so-called pacification campaigns (*Requiem*, p. 192).
[23] Lover, concubine, prostitute. As we can read in the work: 'I was considered the *nona* of the port captain. *Nona* in the Malay language means lady. A peculiar way of saying without saying. Even though everyone knew the exact status. It was the woman who stood on the quay waving her fan while waiting for the next one' (*Requiem*, p. 46).
[24] Samuelson, 'Coastal Form', p. 18.

in geographical terms (quite obvious since it is an island), but also in terms of identity. The novel is thus marked by the 'centrifugal force of the ocean and the centripetal pull of the land'.[25]

Therefore, we believe that Indian Ocean Studies, namely the aesthetic-literary aspects highlighted by Samuelson and Michael N. Pearson's studies on coastal societies, can provide a theoretical framework for some of the aspects in Luís Cardoso's *oeuvre*. By focusing on the insular, coastal and port spaces of Cardoso's narrative, we intend to elaborate critically on the maritime imaginary of this author's narrative.

Over many years dedicated to Indian Ocean historiography, Pearson has expanded the study of coastal societies and port cities, evincing not so much the internal perspective, but their interaction with the sea. For the historian, the littoral is permeable, because it results from the conjunction between land and sea.[26] Another aspect that can help us frame the dynamics of the novel is the idea of connectivity that Pearson retrieves from Horden and Purcell's studies on the Mediterranean. Applying it to the Indian Ocean context, Pearson recalls that the island escapes the stereotype of an isolated and remote place, 'because it has all around connectivity'.[27] As the historian demonstrates, the islands 'are especially accessible to the seaborne, and in a way are coastal area writ large'.[28]

In our view, the above-mentioned aspects related to permeability and connectivity characterize the Timorese territory and the narrative of this novel. Indeed, in this work Timor is not only a meeting point between imperial powers, but also a place where individuals who move from one corner to another of the ocean and continents cross paths. Some of these individuals place themselves at the interstices of hegemonic and historical forces: convicts, travellers, sailors and diasporic characters who, like Catarina, settle on the coast. So, if on the one hand Timor is portrayed as a distant and isolated place, a land of convicts, on the other hand that island is also the place where human and cultural flows converge and intertwine. Thus, Timor becomes the centre of a series of crossings and oceanic routes that dramatically and inevitably mark its history.

Catarina herself is the fruit of the interconnections generated by these coastal and insular spaces in south-east Asia. However, this character, whose initial connection to the sea is due to the crossing she makes to reach Dili, statically waits on the coast, looking at the maritime horizon. Catarina materializes the comings and goings of the land and of the sea.

In this regard, we would like to mention one of the concepts developed by Pearson. In conceptualizing 'the land–sea relation and connections', the historian relies on the image of *ressac* introduced by Jean-Claude Penrad:

---

[25] Samuelson, p. 20.
[26] Michael N. Pearson, 'Littoral Societies: The Concept and the Problem', *Journal of World History*, 17.4, (2006), 353–73 (p. 359).
[27] Pearson, p. 358.
[28] Ibid.

'the threefold violent movement of the waves, turning back on themselves as they crash against the shore'.[29] As Pearson explains with reference to Penrad's concept, 'He uses this image to elucidate the way in which the to-and-fro movements of the Indian Ocean mirror coastal and inland influences that keep coming back at each other just as do waves'.[30]

It seems to us that Catarina's wanderings partly reflect this undulating movement, from the coast to the interior (to visit the coffee plantations) and from the sea to the port, with the arrivals and departures of the various characters and political forces that interact with her. In a sense, Catarina can metaphorically represent this idea of backwash. The inaugural violence is the first sign of that backwash, the balcony is the moment of pause between the two movements, whereas the encounter with the solitary sailor constitutes the other movement that counteracts the first by taking her to water on the sailor's sailboat.

As for the comparison between the backwash and the existential journey, we invite the reader to consider, for instance, the following passage of the text: '[...] as when the sea decides to invade the land. Nothing to do but let yourself go or perhaps cling to a rock, a tree, a lifebuoy until everything returns to its initial state' (*Requiem*, p. 89). The idea of a cycle of opposition, overlap and separation between land and sea, associated with the backwash, seems to mark not only the life of the protagonist, but also that of the country where she resides.

In the first part of this essay, we have analysed some of the metaphorical resources linked to the maritime imaginary. We would now like to address the elements of material culture linked to the sea, since this aspect represents another dimension of Cardoso's literary imaginary.

In addition to a metaphorical dimension, the ocean also carries a material dimension, as illustrated, for example, in the following excerpt in which the narrator evokes the olfactory sensation connected to the port: 'I have always loved ports, places of departure and arrival. Also the ships and the smell of the sandalwood crates where they packed trinkets. A very ingenious way to export the precious wood' (p. 125). Beyond the sense of smell, the text refers to some economic activities linked to the maritime material culture typical of coastal and insular areas, such as the salt pans in Tasi Tolu near Dili and the production of dried fish (referred to in the final part of the work).

Finally, we must address the culinary aspect of the maritime material culture, and specifically the episode of the *saboko* prepared by Madalena, another female character in the novel. The fish for this traditional Timorese dish is caught along the coral by the wise hands of Madalena, who was 'originally from an island where one learned to know the fish as an infant and where one was introduced to the shark ancestors' (p. 76). This passage refers to Madalena's connection to the sea, alluding to a Timorese legend according to

---

[29] Pearson, p. 359.
[30] Pearson, p. 358.

which the ancestors of the inhabitants of Ataúro Island transformed themselves into sharks after their death.

The narration does not simply evoke the dish which contains local ingredients, but it also evokes the symbolism of the fish, which, like any other poisonous one, can cause dizziness and drowsiness, thus providing 'a guaranteed trip to the depths of the ocean where everything is blue as in a limbo' (p. 75). Nevertheless, nothing happens at the first dinner of *saboko*, and Catarina is disappointed to have missed the crossing to the bottom of the sea: 'However I was left with a bittersweet taste on my tongue for not going on this incursion. I know that in life everyone dreams of making a great journey. To that submerged and unknown territory. The resting place of all those who got lost in the Crossing or in Time' (pp. 76–77). But a second dinner does deliver on the promise 'to take a dive to the bottom of the sea' (p. 87) because Catarina 'had always dreamed of going to the bottom of the sea, in a submarine or scuba, or, failing those, the *saboko*' (p. 93). But what is this world of the ocean depths? After evoking the reading of *Twenty Thousand Leagues under the Sea* by Jules Verne (p. 94), the narrator clarifies that the bottom of the sea has to do with existential origin: 'blue [is] the bottom of the sea like my mother's womb' (p. 99).

So, by conjuring up a uterine imaginary associated with the aquatic element and the deepest part of the subconscious, the sea provides an ontological journey to the origins. But if the sea is a place of origin (individual and human, but also mythological should we consider the Timorese case), it is also a place of death, through the torpor of sleepiness induced by the fish and also by the recurring theme of the maritime tomb.

Indeed, the epigraph of the novel quotes the poem 'Visão' by the poet Ruy Cinatti,[31] 'Sepultem-me no mar, longe de tudo' [Bury me at sea, far from it all], evocative of Gerbault's last wish. In this regard, it should be noted that the theme of the maritime tomb is also present in other Portuguese-speaking authors, such as the poet Glória de Sant'Anna who, in Mozambique, facing the Indian Ocean, wrote these verses: 'If I die afar | bury me at sea | inside the ignorant and lucid | seaweed'.[32] In this sense, we can argue that the maritime tomb claims the identity and cultural belonging to the sea and makes it no longer a place of imprisonment, but the place of deepest intimacy and of origins. Just as water epitomizes origin through the womb, so death is equated with the depths of the sea.

The poisoning episode, described above, also involves the topics of the crossing and the journey, and indeed Catarina warns that 'a journey only makes sense if one returns to tell how it was' (p. 88). Such a statement stresses the importance of reporting on the journey, as if only the oral or written

---

[31] Portuguese poet, anthropologist and agronomist (like Cardoso, who studied forestry), who devoted much of his life to the study and visual recording of Timor. The innumerable poetic texts about Timor are a reflection of his experiences, such as the poem cited in the epigraph, dedicated to the French navigator.

[32] Glória de Sant'Anna, *Amaranto: Poesia, 1951–1983* (Lisbon: INCM, 1988), p. 57.

narration could prove the effective accomplishment of the crossing. In this regard, we refer the reader to tales of navigations such as those by Pigafetta, a figure around whom Cardoso builds his subsequent work (2013), or by Alain Gerbault's *À la poursuite du soleil*. Thus, we conclude that the theme of circumnavigation and sea crossing underlies the narrative of this novel. In addition, the two texts by Cardoso, *Requiem for the Solitary Sailor* and *O ano em que Pigafetta completou a circum-navegação* [*The Year Pigafetta Completed the Circumnavigation*], resume in narrative fiction the story of two protagonists of the circumnavigations, Gerbault and Pigafetta.

Regarding the correspondence between Gerbault's circumnavigation and that of Magellan, we invite the reader to consider the passage in which Catarina, so curious to obtain more details about the solitary sailor, claims not to know the story of Ferdinand Magellan (p. 89). Later, she summarizes the navigator's feats in a few sentences: 'I did not know the story of the first man who made the first voyage of circumnavigation. [...] The locals gave him no time to escape. They cut off his head thinking he was also looking for the sun' (p. 89).

If, on the one hand, we find a possible correspondence between Gerbault's and Magellan's enterprises, on the other hand we are left wondering how these circumnavigations engage with Catarina's crossing on the Timorese island. In fact, *Requiem for the Solitary Sailor* metaphorically weaves the crossing of the main character, Catarina, and at the same time engages intertextually with narratives that allude to the topics of maritime voyages and crossings. It is in this context that we should read Cinatti's epigraph, which, as we have seen, summons the solitary sailor's desire to be buried at sea, far from everything. Part of the verse quoted in the epigraph is resumed in the third person at the end of the novel, thus materializing in the text the circular path of circumnavigation and of life, as origin and death converge in the depths of the sea. In fact, at the end of the novel Alain Gerbault's sailboat finally reaches Dili, but the sailor, now sick, having managed to see the sun rise on the sea horizon and having asked Catarina to bury him at sea, passes away.

After the death of the sailor and following the fire that has destroyed the house where she lived, Catarina moves to the sailboat. Thus, the woman from Batavia finds in Gerbault's sailboat her 'castle built on the sea' (p. 201). Further ahead, the narrator reaffirms her strong connection to the sea: 'the only place where I felt safe was at sea. On the French navigator's sailboat' (p. 203). Catarina will only leave the sailboat after having written her logbook (p. 208). It is an elaboration of the crossing itself, an account of what she witnessed during the terrible times of the war, a memoir comparable to the logbook that told of Gerbault's solitary voyage of circumnavigation (p. 208). These memories cast a peculiar perspective on Timor's history. In addition, the logbook becomes an act that subverts the double silencing of the protagonist (resuming the concept of double colonization).

As remarked by Silva, 'the diasporic scene of writings [...] offers alternatives

[sic] narratives of Empire and the problematic figures embedded therein'.[33] In this respect, it seems to us particularly interesting that the person who collects the memories in the logbook and rejoins the fragments of Timorese history is an oriental woman who places herself at the interstices of the colonial powers with which she is somehow forced to interact. Despite not being Timorese, Catarina embraces some of the cultural customs of the local population (as is the case of food, clothing — the *tais fetu* — and some rituals, such as the *masca*, p. 174), speaks French as if she were a Parisian, and Tetum as if she were a Timorese (p. 166). In doing so she sews together different cultural identities, exposing the inevitable interaction that takes place between the multiple forces operating in the Timorese territory.

At the end of the novel, after the departure of the Japanese troops and the recovery of Portuguese colonial power with the arrival of the ghost ship whose crossing had lasted an entire war (p. 218), the port captain invites Catarina to leave the island, saying 'We should leave to forget everything, the war, the deaths, and go out to sea', but she declines the offer: 'I reminded him that the French navigator's sailboat was at his disposal. I had already made my solitary crossing during the war. I recorded everything in my logbook. I planned to stay on land' (p. 222).

Through Catarina, the novel looks at Timorese history at the beginning of the Second World War, recalling times marked by oppression and consecutive invasions. The text provides multifocal perspectives on the dramatic events of history, through the gaze of the female narrator and protagonist. Such a perspective also extends to the geographical space of the novel, in a perpetual game between land and sea, the balcony and the ocean, the coast and the inland mountains, the reality of the present and the dream. It is in this context that the inside–outside dichotomy is fragmented by the gaze of Catarina, someone who constantly moves between these two categories. The protagonist's vision is comparable to the coastal form, a link between land and sea, a look from the balcony that foretells the future or hope.

The littoral, as observed by Samuelson, 'exceeds an idiom of in-betweenness and liminality even as it seems to materialize these states: rather than being between land and sea, the littoral is an ecotone in which the elements of earth and water ceaselessly overlap and draw apart'.[34] Catarina moves between worlds and worldviews that overlap and draw apart; she is not a local inhabitant, but neither is she part of the oppressive forces. In this sense, the protagonist is, as defined by another character in the book, 'a privileged observer' (p. 208), someone who inhabits the space of the coast, between land and sea.

In short, considering that the balcony, the coast, the sailboat, and the port, among other elements analysed here, all fit into a prolific maritime and coastal imaginary, we can conclude that the insular geography of this novel creates

---

[33] Silva, p. 148.
[34] Samuelson, p. 17.

a specific literary aesthetic. In fact, we believe that the sea and the Timorese coast are not merely the background to this novel but provide an aesthetic imaginary that Samuelson calls 'littoral literature'.[35] The seafront balcony, one of the most significant locations in this approach to littoral literature, is the place from where Catarina is allowed to project her dreams onto the maritime horizon. The solitary navigator's sailboat, where the protagonist writes her logbook, can also be considered an extension of the littoral space, since it is a floating space anchored to land. But it is especially in the wanderings of the protagonist between the port and the balcony and in the metaphors that represent Catarina's crossing that we find the realization of a possible littoral literature. In this regard, we invite the reader to peruse the following passage in which the protagonist summarizes her own life experience in Timor:

> I landed on an island known as the place where the sun rose, although nobody knew the exact place. Even farther east than the East. On the line where the land ends and the sea begins, and at the moment when the Sea-Man blends with the Sea-Woman. I was stranded like a ship that had been damaged by crashing into a coral reef. No one came to my rescue. (p. 179)

The passage refers to Catarina's crossing to Timor, drawing on the maritime metaphor of the ship stranded on the coast. In addition, the narrator mentions the point of union between *tasi feto* [sea woman] and *tasi mane* [sea man], that is, between the north coast and the south coast of Timor.

In conclusion, as we have seen throughout this essay, the insular geography and the theme of the crossing mark the imagery of this narrative, drawing on maritime metaphors to define the narrator's existential journey. Moreover, in the echoes of the circumnavigation voyages, this novel casts a look at the history of the country, since Catarina experiences the historical dynamics of this territory as one who observes the processes of coastal erosion and sedimentation: consecutive occupations, arrivals and departures, flows of individuals who interact among themselves and, at the same time, change the configuration of this island. Thus, the coastal and insular imaginary as well as the maritime journey lie at the origin of this narrative, not only for the metaphors that evoke these spaces, but also for the perception of life as a crossing.

At the end of the novel, Catarina's determination to keep her feet firmly on the land, but with her gaze open to the plenitude of the maritime horizon, keeps alive the hope of being reunited with her kidnapped son who, like a castaway (p. 222), would recognize the lamp lit by his mother. It is on the Timorese island, between the mountains and the sea, that we will find the adventures of Catarina's son, in the ensuing novel by Luís Cardoso.

---

[35] Samuelson, p. 16.

Reviews

PAMILA GUPTA, *Portuguese Decolonization in the Indian Ocean World: History and Ethnography* (London: Bloomsbury, 2019). 225 pages. Print and ebook.

Reviewed by PAUL MELO E CASTRO (University of Glasgow)

A recent growth area in postcolonial studies has involved what one might loosely describe as 'oceanic perspectives'. The attractions are obvious, in that such perspectives effectively provincialize Europe as one point in a network of exchanges and allow for a renovation of existing topics by recovering interconnections between former colonial spaces that a more national(ist) focus might occlude. Given that the bulk of Portuguese speakers are located around the South Atlantic and that a significant number, if not the majority, are of at least partial African descent, it is no surprise that Paul Gilroy's Black Atlantic paradigm of a 'counterculture of modernity' emerging in the wake of the middle passage has provided the main inspiration within Lusophone Studies. Lately however, as attested by such works as Fernando Rosa's *The Portuguese in the Creole Indian Ocean* (2015), among various articles and research projects, interest has also grown in how Isabel Hofmeyr's countervailing Indian Ocean paradigm — in which processes of exchange long predate colonial modernity, even if increased and then informed by it — might bring about studies of the peripheral, less integrated, even residual eastern territories of the former Portuguese empire, stretching from Mozambique to India and onwards to Timor Leste. It to this emergent debate that Pamela Gupta's *Portuguese Decolonization in the Indian Ocean World* contributes, asking some searching questions of an original variety of ethnographic materials and historical junctures yet equally showing the risks that working across such a broad scope may entail.

Gupta has done a significant amount to introduce the Indian Ocean paradigm, being *inter alia* one of the editors of *Eyes across the Water: Navigating the Indian Ocean* (2010). The present work collects a series of articles written subsequently and linking Angola, South Africa, Mozambique and Goa through the lens of decolonization, which the author pegs to two dates: 1961, when Goa was annexed by India, and 1975, when Angola and Mozambique achieved independence after the Carnation Revolution in Portugal. While 1975 is uncontroversial, whether 1961 represented decolonization or recolonization is a tricky subject, as the various debates put forward by Goa's Al-Zulaij Collective show.

One of this book's main points of interest is the wide variety of subjects it traverses, taking in references to the work of Ryszard Kapuściński, Mia Couto and Ricardo Rangel alongside the life stories of the Goan fishing community of Catembe and White Portuguese Africans who left Angola and Mozambique for South Africa. Decolonization becomes a way of discussing the messiness of lives that continued through traumatic breaks in the historical timeline. The section on 'retornados' (if I can bend the meaning of this word so much, though many of the 'retornados' to Portugal were hardly returning there either) in South Africa is fascinating, the most interesting in the book for me. We see how this exodus, which has been given less attention than the high-profile flux of Whites to Portugal, was driven by a complex mix of self-identification as white Africans and the desire to preserve the prestige that colonial status brought. The fine-grained discussion of these lives is neatly complemented by the inclusion of photographs by Ricardo Rangel detailing the 1975 settler exodus from Lourenço Marques, adding a contrasting viewpoint to the memories of the interviewees. The section on Goans in Mozambique is equally interesting, the interviewees' recollection of their ambivalent entanglements with whiteness and blackness exemplifying what Cristiana Bastos, quoted, calls their 'floating position'.

When problems arise, it is often in point of detail and partly through the cursory treatment given some issues. Here for brevity I focus on two subjects I know something of. Can we simply discuss Ricardo Rangel's photographs as 'visual metaphors'? Does the analysis of such documentary photography not have to engage with its claims on reality as trace or metonymy? What proof is there that many of Rangel's colonial-era photographs were destroyed by the Portuguese colonial state, rather than their publication simply being suppressed in the normal run of censorship? And which ones? It is worth recalling that Rangel was fêted by the authorities to the point of having a solo retrospective at the tail end of colonial rule. At one point, discussing one of Rangel's photographs showing a family of Goan fishermen at home, the author wonders if the partially visible legs and feet (in polished shoes) belong to the husband or father of the household. In fact, the negative of this image held at the Centro de Documentação e Formação Fotográfica in Maputo shows this figure to be white, almost certainly the journalist Mendes de Oliveira, with whom Rangel worked on the story 'Pescadores de Catembe' for the newsmagazine *Tempo* in 1972 and which features this image slightly cropped to remove the distracting appendages. It would have enhanced Gupta's account, rich in impressionism, to have looked at how professional duties as well as subjective interests led Rangel's image-making.

As regards Portuguese India, did it really come to 'a quiet end'? Not for those on both sides who lost their lives in the brief conflict. There are various problems of detail in the hasty historical accounts contextualizing the various chapters. The newspaper *O Heraldo* was not founded by Luís de Menezes Bragança, but by Aleixo Messias Gomes, and it was far from the first Goan newspapers to criticize the colonial state. Nehru did not organize the 1946 pro-India rally in Margão (which, being a good four miles from the nearest beach, can hardly be described as 'a port city in Goa'). It was organized by Julião

Menezes, who invited Ram Lohia to speak (for which Menezes was arrested). Did Angola really have the second biggest European settler population in Africa by the mid-nineteenth century? Bigger than Algeria, which had at least 50,000 white residents by 1847? Perhaps these examples show the difficulty of working across such varied contexts. Susan Stanford Friedman argues that comparison, by its very nature, tracks away from the 'thick description' required for what Clifford Geertz terms 'local knowledge'. The further we range and the more far-flung connections we wish to make, the higher the entry tariff in terms of contextual knowledge.

Skating across context in this way also brings the danger of drifting from one's sources. Gupta refers to Sousa Santos describing how Portuguese settlers in Mozambique chose to intermarry with Goans over Black Africans. Yet on the page referenced there is no mention of Goans. The only such mention in Sousa Santos's text is a quote from António Pinto Miranda, of 1766, decrying that Europeans in Mozambique 'marry local ladies and others of Goan descent' and, in so doing, 'forget their Christian upbringing'. For Miranda, marriage to Goans drove 'cafrealização', not Goan equiparation with the colonizer. And it is not only written sources that should have been consulted with more care. While interesting enough, the short film 'Beira' that is referenced from Youtube — and which consists of old photographs set to pop music — is not a work by the celebrated Mozambican photographer Filipe Branquinho, one of the leading lights in the nation's contemporary arts scene, but by a similarly named blogger, apparently resident in Portugal, identified on the video-sharing platform as F. J. Branquinho de Almeida. The video is in fact an example of the intense, and often problematically rose-tinted, amateur memorialization of Africa that has attracted much critical attention in Portugal. Many such small problems crop up throughout the book. Though in themselves they do not necessarily undermine the global points, they do raise some questions about the soundness of the conclusions. Would they befall a study that, in dealing with individual subjects, was not in such a hurry to get *elsewhere*? One might pose a similar question about some claims for the exceptionalism of the subject and the originality of the focus, which is stated more than substantiated. Was Portuguese colonialism 'uniquely itinerant' for example (p. 11)? It's not clear to me that British or French colonialism were less itinerant, as Gandhi's travels from India to England to South Africa or Fanon's movement from Martinique to France to Algeria attest, just to name two well-known trajectories.

In short, *Portuguese Decolonization* shows both the possibilities and dangers that attend an oceanic perspective, the wide vistas that open up between ports of call, but also the attendant skerries of detail upon which we risk running aground and the perils of losing sight of land.

ELENA BRUGIONI, ORLANDO GROSSEGESSE and PAULO DE MEDEIROS (eds), *A Companion to João Paulo Borges Coelho: Rewriting the (Post)Colonial Remains* (Oxford: Peter Lang, 2020). vi + 266 pages. Print and ebook.

Reviewed by HILARY OWEN (University of Oxford)

This collection stands out as the first full-length work in English to bring the works of Borges Coelho to the critical reader in the anglosphere, complementing important article-length studies to date by scholars such as Stefan Helgesson. It presents us with an English translation of a short story by the Mozambican author and historian, João Paulo Borges Coelho, followed by nine chapters covering almost all of his published works of fiction. Offering an extremely rich array of themes and approaches, this volume performs a complex and demanding twofold task with efficacy and style. Firstly, the editors make an irrefutable case for regarding Borges Coelho as the talented, transnationally resonant contemporary writer that he is, reaching far beyond Mozambican literature to the interface of Portuguese-language writing with the global, world-literature scene. Secondly, the nine authors in this work effectively demonstrate how Borges Coelho's trajectory as a professional historian, a craftsman of creative fiction and a bearer of twentieth-century (post)colonial memory invites ongoing engagement with the trends that have shaped critical and theoretical thinking on (post)colonialism, poststructuralism, world-literature and world capitalist systems over the last thirty years. While a substantial body of high-quality research exists on Borges Coelho in Portuguese, there is markedly less available in English. And in terms of translation into English, his work has been far outflanked by his countryman, Mozambique's most canonical author, Mia Couto. While comparison with Couto might have been one obvious direction in which to take the current project, it is a definite and notable plus that none of the contributors has yielded to this temptation. Borges Coelho is rightly allowed to speak here entirely and brilliantly as his own man. His work is, like Couto's, highly sensitive to the construction of Africa's archives through the optic of a European language worldview, and this sensitivity is omnipresent in his work. However, while this affords Couto a rich vein of spontaneous poetic invention through hybridizations of African oral culture and Portuguese scripted sign, Borges Coelho is far less inclined to privilege Portuguese language as national metonym in the transcultural contact zone. The prose style which results is refreshingly readable and highly accessible, without sacrifice of self-reflexivity, political sophistication or ethical rigour.

The Introduction to the volume provides a valuable overview not only, as is customary, of the individual chapters but also of the full literary *oeuvre* of Borges Coelho. This helps to situate what follows and the short plot summaries offer a useful diachronic mapping of the author's evolving direction. This is followed by a beautiful new English translation by David Brookshaw of Borges Coelho's short story 'O pano encantado'. Aside from the obvious delight of having this inclusion from a master translator of African literature in Portuguese, this serves as an unambiguous endorsement of the fact that we need to see more of Borges Coelho's work in English, a point to which I will return.

Chapter 2, by Paolo Israel, takes the unconventional but useful step of focusing on Borges Coelho's professional career as a historian in the highly politicized context of knowledge production in Marxist-Leninist Mozambique, starting with his time working for TBARN (Centro de Estudos de Técnicas Básicas para o Aproveitamento dos Recursos Naturais) under the aegis of Aquino de Bragança's famous Centro de Estudos Africanos (CEA) Universidade Eduardo Mondlane. Covering the late 1970s through to the 1990s, this chapter includes a fascinating foray into Borges Coelho's early experiments with comic strips and 'graphic novels'. Israel also makes us very aware of the subsequent difficulties which beset preservation, access and retrieval in respect of the material archive, encouraging us to view Borges Coelho's decision to write postmodern historiographic metafiction in terms of a largely pragmatic choice, driven by his frustration with the archive's obstructions and limitations. Finally, Israel's chapter neatly establishes the possibility of grounding the eight chapters which follow in a specific biographical and historical context.

Continuing from the vantage point of overview, Chapter 3, by Nazir Ahmed Can, gives a reading of Borges Coelho's first six novels, pursuing the connecting thread of literary experimentation, diversification and the interrogation of historiographic silences as the key to understanding both his ethical commitment to local memory, and the degree of aesthetic renovation and invigoration which he brings to the Mozambican literary scene.

Chapter 4, by Ana Mafalda Leite, is a standout piece in the volume. Leite undertakes a finely honed reading of narrative itself as a medium of transit connecting the Indian Ocean's islands, shores and liminal spaces. She draws on Borges Coelho's essay 'O Índico como lugar', to show how his conceptualization of *spiritu loci* in his two short story collections, *Índicos Indícios I* and *II*, foregrounds the idea of shorelines being viewed from the sea in a blended textuality of the littoral, where history, myth and parable form overlapping, often deconstructive, layers.

Chapter 5, by Rui Gonçalves Miranda, continues with this Indian Ocean thematic, this time in relation to a single short story from *Índicos Indícios II*, 'A força do mar de agosto'. This narrative is intricately read here in a classic deconstructive critique of neoliberal authoritarianism, drawing particularly effectively on Jacques Rancière's *The Names of History: On the Poetics of Knowledge*, to bring out the fluidity and porosity which unmake that which is conventionally 'nation-bound'. Maintaining dialogues also with Jules Michelet, Achille Mbembe and Hayden White, the chapter goes on to explore the peculiar contact zones of surface, depth and commerce which are physically enacted by the sea in and as history, as well as being textually encoded here in Borges Coelho's proposal of a new oceanographic aesthetic of reading and writing.

Miranda finishes the piece with a brilliant insight from Derrida's *Glas*, in which reading is an act of dredging and scraping the bottom of the sea in a homophonic French pun which plays on 'la mer' and 'la mère'. In this context, Miranda leaves open the tempting question of what is lost (or gained?) when Derrida's overt maternal feminization of the maritime, in his words 'You do not catch the sea. She always reforms herself', is transposed into the gender neutral 'it', as occurs here in Miranda's concluding paraphrase, 'you do not catch the sea. It always reforms itself' (pp. 127–29).

Chapter 6, by Jessica Falconi, brings us an entertaining and sharply focused reading of the tourist gaze, drawing on critical tourism studies in the humorous short fiction work, *Hinyambaan: novela burlesca*. Here Falconi shows us how Borges Coelho parodically discloses South Africa's ongoing racialization of the 'other space' and the 'other collective group' as his two South African tourist families ironically and unwittingly 'auto-exoticize' their own gaze, thus exposing the racist projections of their own internal social and knowledge hierarchies, during their annual road-trip vacation in Mozambique. Her astute interpretation of the micro-relations between characters as being indicative of the macro-relations between South Africa and Mozambique, and also of the local and the global, not only works on its own terms, but also effectively paves the way for the remaining chapters of this volume. All of these, in different ways, locate Borges Coelho in more overtly transnational, universal, cosmopolitan or 'world-literary' frames.

Chapter 7, by Orlando Grossegesse, gives a meticulous comparative reading of *O Olho de Hertzog* alongside Christian Kracht's 2012 novel *Imperium*. In addition to their roughly coincident early twentieth-century timelines, Grossegesse points out that both works felicitously share a focus on the German longwave wireless station established by Telefunken at Nauen, near Berlin, in 1905, enabling German colonial communications to bypass British control. This common field of literal and metaphorical reference inspires Grossegesse to discuss the ways in which both novels critique the geopolitical and historical frameworks which a global-imperial communication network makes visible. Drawing on Linda Hutcheon's paradigm of historiographic metafiction, Grossegesse shows Borges Coelho deploying a counterfactual logic of difference to expose the eurocentricity of dominant historiographies, pursuing a direction which shifts his literary focus onto overtly cosmopolitan terrain. In conclusion, Grossegesse argues that Borges Coelho ultimately takes this model of geopolitical fiction 'beyond a break with Eurocentrism and a shift to the Indian Ocean' (p. 173), so that the novel's 'spacetime' is rethought in terms of a global connectedness that is emblematized by Mozambique itself as a universalist merging of civilizations.

In Chapter 8, Elena Brugioni takes a formalist-inspired approach to *Rainhas da Noite*, and its narrative dialogue between literary fiction and history, through four specific indicators: traces, clues, archiving and witnessing, with a particular emphasis on the epistemologies of knowledge production and their relation to cultural memory. This chapter also therefore affords an interesting link with Chapter 3 by Nazir Ahmed Can. Brugioni's piece makes a case, via Reinhart Koselleck's *Futures Past*, for seeing those unofficial, subjective microhistories of empire which foreground lived experiences outside and against the teleologies of historical record, as a move to show literary representation itself challenging the knowledge production processes which consolidate history and tradition.

Chapter 9, by Emanuelle Santos, continues the exploration of *Rainhas da Noite* in relation to a transnational perspective on postcolonial memory, making an assured and confident case for situating this novel in the wider sphere of world-literary aesthetics. For Santos, the power relations which make up the intrigue of *Rainhas da Noite* are played out in the always internationalized colonial networks of British, Belgian and Portuguese mining interests, and in the shifting hierarchies which these networks produced in the world-capitalist system. This opens the novel's 'minor' histories onto a global politics of postcolonial memory.

Paulo de Medeiros's highly compelling and timely final chapter takes as its inspiration the 'water' politics, flooding and drought experiences that are shared by the novel *Ponta Gea* and the novella, *Água: uma novela rural*. Medeiros deploys concepts debated by the Warwick Research Collective, and their working definition of world-literature as the literature of 'the world-system, of the modern capitalist world-system, that is' (p. 223) to advance a materialist-informed but also incisively formalist reading of Borges Coelho's allegorical take on ecology, climate change, memory and technology. Medeiros's analysis carefully unpacks the metanarrative weave of allegorical structuring and magical realism which runs through these two works. He ultimately connects both texts in terms of how they treat antinomies, including temporal ones, as fluid, noting the 'aquatic' dissolution of past and present boundaries, as well as observing that both works invite, indeed require, us to reflect on the role that massive developmental inequality plays in the current march of climate catastrophe.

Given the sheer depth, breadth and critical *richesse* of the readings which make up this volume, it is probably fair to say that the editors undersell their own achievement when they write as follows: 'in spite of, or rather thanks to, the many changes and adjustments the project underwent along the way, the book represents what we view as a strong contribution to scholarship on the work of João Paulo Borges Coelho' (p. 3). Admittedly, the book does not cover the whole of Borges Coelho's published output, but it does feel much more structured and planned than the above statement allows for. Even chapters which focus on the same works, such as 4 and 5 on *Índicos Indícios* or 3, 8 and 9 covering *Rainhas da Noite*, still afford enlightening cross-references rather than mere repetition. The outcome of this project is well-named as a 'companion'. A *vade mecum* in the most positive sense, it is likely to remain *the* anglophone companion for a long time to come, and will be indispensable for undergraduate and taught MA courses on Lusophone Studies programmes. Given that the collection offers high-quality secondary reading in English, it also now becomes possible to include Borges Coelho in Comparative and World Literature courses taught in the anglosphere. Evidently, what needs to come next is widescale translation of Borges Coelho's works into English. And it is very much to be hoped that these fine critical studies will help to expedite that process.

KRISTIAN VAN HAESENDONCK (ed.), *The Worlds of Mia Couto* (Oxford: Peter Lang, 2020), vii + 180 pages. Print and ebook.

Reviewed by MARTA BANASIAK (University of Campinas (UNICAMP)/ FAPESP — postdoctoral research grant no. 2020/03902-9)

Mia Couto is, without any doubt or exaggeration, the flagship writer of the so-called African literatures in the Portuguese language. He is usually the first one to be read by those who become interested in these literatures. He is also the most translated and his work is analysed, at least once in a lifetime, by the vast majority of researchers in African literatures in Portuguese. In fact, my case was no different as my first publication was also dedicated to one of Mia Couto's novels. Within such an immense theoretical production on the work of this writer, I would distinguish three or four main thematic lines that usually permeate a large part of the academic texts related to Mia Couto's books: the influence of orality, 'tradition', the construction of 'Mozambicanity', as well as infinite dissections of his linguistic inventions. This, in my view, caused a kind of saturation and, consequently, a stagnation in studies of Couto's work. Therefore, it was with great joy and excitement that I received the proposal to review a book that, as its editor Kristian Van Haesendonck states in the introduction, 'aims to create a dialogue between the number of experts in order to lift the writer out of his linguistic and national — Mozambican — confinement, opening up the study of his work to an increasingly globalized world and the inevitable debate on World Literature'. However, great excitement always goes hand in hand with great expectations. Does the book deliver what it promises?

The book, published by Peter Lang in 2020, is a product of the workshop under the same title organized by Van Haesendonck within the Postcolonial Literature Research Group at the University of Antwerp in May 2017. The book is divided into three parts entitled 'Worlding Mia Couto', 'Mia Couto's Worlds' and 'Mixing Wor(l)ds'. Apart from the final part, which contains the editor's interview with Mia Couto, each of the other two parts is composed of four texts, those in Part I being of a more theoretical nature, proposing new theoretical frameworks and new ways of thinking about Couto's work, while Part II contains texts that propose new readings of particular novels, both older and more recent. The texts are authored by researchers of five nationalities, from seven European and US universities, a fact that, on the one hand, allows the book to be read as a dialogue between experts, as announced by the editor. On the other, however, it is a dialogue that clearly privileges Western academia.

The first part of the book is framed by the first and last texts which propose new theoretical placements for Couto's work, while those in the middle offer less canonical views on the writer's working with the language. In the first essay, Paulo de Medeiros proposes to look at Couto within the paradigm of world-literature developed by the Warwick Research Collective in order to observe the process of reshaping world-literature from the periphery. He focuses on the social-political role of literature, taking into account the context of world capitalism rather than the national context. It is an approach that, in my view, traces the paths for the participatory future of African literatures in the world context. In the last essay of this part, Peter J. Maurits also addresses the functioning of the world-system and places Mia Couto's novel *O Outro Pé da Sereia* [*The Mermaid's Other Foot*] in the context of global aesthetics and compares it with Alejandro González Iñárritu's film *Babel*. Despite the fact that *O Outro Pé da Sereia* appears visibly less 'global' than the film it is compared to, the essay, in addition to the fact that it analytically joins different languages of artistic expression in a productive way, undoubtedly traces new paths for thinking about Couto's work.

The first text on the language, and the second in the book, is by David Brookshaw. In this essay, by comparing the language constructed by Mia Couto with two other writers from other postcolonial spaces, the scholar introduces the concept of diaspora understood as the autonomous territory of imagination and creativity. In this sense, the text proposes a move away from the political space towards the intimate — the terrain that is still little explored in African literatures. However, it is the third text of the book 'Mia Couto and his African Context: Invention of an Origin', by Ewa A. Łukaszyk, which caused me some concern. On the one hand, the text brings something that we could call freshness, mainly due to its non-celebratory tone in relation to Couto and the approach taken to issues of racial origin rarely discussed by researchers. On the other hand, the text seems to be based on one assumption already incorporated in the title, namely that Mia Couto in his writing intends to build a language that represents some imaginary Mozambicanity. This idea permeates the argumentation presented in the essay leading to an attempt to prove that the writer fails in this project, like in the claim that '[n]o matter how far he seems to go on the path of deconstructing the Portuguese language, Couto remains a writer of the Lusophony. His experiments in exploring the synergy of Portuguese and Bantu languages set him quite close to the old utopia of the post-Babelian reconstruction' (p. 58). With this, in my opinion, very hasty thesis, the otherwise very sophisticated essay doesn't fully deliver its promises.

The second section of the book is no less interesting than the first, containing two essays dedicated to the writer's earliest novels and two dedicated to his more recent work. The opening essay, which is perhaps the best in this part of the book, Kamila Krakowska Rodrigues analyses the appropriation and deconstruction of the intertexts of the ethnographic classics of Henri Junod and Theodor Koch-Grunberg in the process of (re)construction of the new national identities in *Terra Somnambula* [*Sleepwalking Land*] and Mario de Andrade's Brazilian modernist classic *Macunaíma*. This essay seems to bridge the gap with the final essay, where Fernanda Vilar observes the process of (re)construction of memory through the contestation of European written sources in the trilogy about the Emperor of Gaza, Ngungunyane. Celina Martins, in her analysis of *A Varanda do Frangipani* [*Under the Frangipani*], unveils the problematics of rhizomatic identities focusing on the non-human element, the frangipani tree. Finally, Irene Marques addresses issues of female resistance and patriarchy, both in traditional African societies and among the colonizing element, in the novel *Mulheres de Cinza* [*Women of Ashes*]. It seems to me that there is a rather problematic contradiction in the text. Throughout the reading I had a feeling that the literary text was treated as a historical document, ignoring the fact that the black female voices are constructed by the white male writer. What is surprising is that Marques even quotes Tom Stennett when he points to this fact, but then dismisses it as an unfair attack on the writer without, in my opinion, problematizing the issue enough.

In any case, aside from the few problematic aspects in some of the essays I pointed out above, I have no doubt that the book fulfills the promise made by its editor in the introduction. It is a publication that truly introduces a fresh look at Mia Couto's literary production. It is also significant that it is a publication in English, something that not only signals the growing interest in the author's work outside the 'Lusophony', but also proves the comparative capacity of his work and its worldwide versatility. Finally, it can be concluded that *The Worlds of Mia Couto* is an indispensable reference for Couto studies in the third decade of the twenty-first century.

WReC — WARWICK RESEARCH COLLECTIVE, *Desenvolvimento combinado e desigual: por uma nova teoria da literatura-mundial*, trans. by Gabriela Beduschi Zanfelice (Campinas: Editora da Unicamp, 2020). 344 pages. Print.

Reviewed by EMANUELLE SANTOS (University of Birmingham)

The Brazilian translation of the 2015 book by Warwick Research Collective (WReC) into Portuguese marks a certain *volta pra casa* of a way of thinking literature in a rather *Tieta*-esque fashion: seasoned on the flavours and ways of the cosmopolitan British academia and holding a certain *altivez*, an all too common undertone of the type of theory produced in the comparative literature — especially at the cores of the world-system. This translation opens to the Portuguese-speaking world an outstanding incursion on the territory of theoretical enquiry in comparative literary studies whose central premises depart from experiences of our own. The WReC's conceptualization of world-literature as the literature that registers the single but radically uneven capitalist world-system in its form and content, relies on the alignment, or superposition, of two fundamental critical paradigms whose theorization is intrinsically linked to the Portuguese-speaking world: Immanuel Wallerstein's world-systems theory, informed by the author's extensive work on the liberation struggles in Portuguese-speaking Africa together with Aquino de Bragança; and Roberto Schwarz's articulation of literary form as *conteúdo sócio-histórico decantado* stemming from the critic's thinking on Brazilian literature, especially through the work of Machado de Assis.

The result is a necessarily dense book whose dialectical relationship between form and content does not betray its critical hypothesis, thus posing a great translation challenge that Gabriela Beduschi Zanfelice has carried out with responsibility and competence. One of the characteristics of the work is the carving of a new terminology needed in order to fulfil the title's promise of a 'nova teoria da literatura-mundial', putting the strategic and careful use of language at the centre of the argument. The hyphen in the WReC's rendition of world-literature turns it into a concept that is radically different from the popular unhyphenated rendition of world literature; similarly, the view of literary form as a registration of world-systemic unevenness goes beyond the idea of literary representation as commonly employed. In this context, the translator shows a commitment to her role as co-creator of critical terminology, achieving a final product that lives up to the terminological refinement of the work, now available in Portuguese.

Notwithstanding these qualities, it would not come as a surprise if a reader were to think that the translation does not flow as well as they think it should, and to this reader I would say that the original in English does not flow easily either. As the result of a collaborative thinking and writing process undertaken by a collective — which go the extra collective mile in this translation, where the list of its members' names that was printed in the original is nowhere to be found — *Desenvolvimento Combinado e Desigual* 'poderia certamente ser denominado desigual e combinado' in terms of its internal organization (p. 16). Aside from the short but extremely useful preface to the Brazilian edition signed by Elena Brugioni, Alfredo Cesar Melo and Paulo de Medeiros, and the Collective's own 'Nota sobre o método colaborativo', the six chapters that follow encompass a range of forms including essays on theory, single-text critical analysis, author-focused analysis and multi-text, multi-author transnational analysis. While the theory proposed and texts chosen are clearly and admittedly prose fiction of varied lengths, the geographic range is wide enough to make a case for a world-systemic argument. Analytical chapters focus on Sudan, Russia, Slovakia, Spain, Iceland, Scotland and South Africa. The theoretical chapters focus on a myriad of exemplary canonical novels from across the globe, with emphasis on Machado de Assis in the light of the theorization by Schwarz but also engaging with the works by the 'three Marias', Maria Isabel Barreno, Maria Teresa Horta and Maria Velho da Costa, Lobo Antunes and Pepetela, to name those commonly associated with Portuguese studies.

Together, the first two chapters constitute roughly half of the volume. The first chapter, titled 'Literatura-mundial no contexto do desenvolvimento combinado e desigual' is an extremely accomplished essay on the wider field of world literature and a robust proposition of world-literature as an analytical category in comparative literary studies. The text's necessary density is due to what reads as an honest commitment to disclose the Collective's political and ideological agenda by openly engaging with their sources, discussing influences and views of the world wherein they locate the literature analysed and their own critical intervention. The heavily (and helpfully) footnoted text does an excellent job situating the WReC's critical position in the international debate on the idea of world literature vis-à-vis the work of other prominent names in the field, welcoming any newcomer to the discussion. The second chapter, titled 'A questão do realismo periférico', engages with theories on the novel by Franco Moretti, explains the necessity of the dialogue with Wallerstein's world-systems theory and through its engagement with the work of Lukács, Adorno and Jameson's concept of singular modernity enters into a sophisticated discussion of peripheral realism that is informed by work of Roberto Schwarz and Michael Löwy's concept of critical irrealism.

The four analytical chapters that follow compose what can be seen as the second half of the book, and promote a combined and uneven picture of the phenomena that the analytical category of world-literature registers in its form and content. Chapter 3, '"Irrealismo" em *Tempo de Migrar para o Norte* de Tayeb Salih' offers a deep-dive into this work of the Sudanese author in the light of Löwy's concept of critical realism that pulls together many of the critical threads guiding the argument in the first half of the book.

In Chapter 4, 'Espectros de *Oboroten*: Licantropia, Neoliberalismo e a Nova Rússia em Victor Pelevin', the WReC depart from Stephen Shapiro's linkage of the re-emergence of gothic narrative devices with recurring cycles of long-wave capitalist accumulation to analyse the emergence of narrative devices associated with the supernatural in post-Soviet Russian fiction. The chapters' argument associating a certain spectral aesthetics to the rise of highly uneven forms of neoliberal capitalism in post-socialist societies', especially those relying heavily on the revenues of petro-economy and/or other types of extractivist economic activities shows itself useful to those looking at selected works in Angolan and Mozambican fiction.

Chapter 5, 'A periferia literária europeia' is essential for those in the studies of literatures in Portuguese who are interested in the place occupied by literary works from Portugal in the Collective's proposition of world-literature. The literary case studies encompass works from Slovakia, Spain, Iceland and Scotland. Despite not analysing any specific works rooted in the Portuguese context, the chapter does a good job in emphasizing the flexible and relational character of categories such as core and periphery, and successfully shows how they are still useful as a way to understand unevenness working within Europe.

Finally, Chapter 6, 'Ivan Vladislavic: Atravessando a cidade desigual', takes us to post-apartheid South Africa in the paradigmatic context of Johannesburg to show how the themes and forms of Vladislavic's work dialogue with the historical and material paradoxes and contradictions that make the systemic unevenness of the world-system in the life of the city. The city-centred approach of systemic concerns of this essay constitutes yet another point of contact with critical traditions in the Portuguese-speaking world that could prove fruitful to the field.

Together, all the chapters of the volume constitute a challenging and highly interesting piece of literary theory that brings a critical verve concerned with real economic, social and historical issues into the heart of the debates around world literature, of which it seems to currently have been washed away. While far from perfect in its re-centring of capitalism rather than on the other systems social and economic organization with which it unevenly combines, lack of engagement with forms other than the novel, and absence of a robust methodological discussion involving choice of corpus and collaborative method, the study is an essential materialist contribution to the field. I, therefore, commend the Kaliban — Centro de Pesquisa em Estudos Pós-Coloniais e Literatura Mundial da Unicamp for making the translation of this work into Portuguese possible, and am confident that the discussions it brings will find fertile terrain in the studies of literatures in Portuguese, as, at the end of the day it also a little bit where it came from.

Abstracts

The Indian Ocean as a Transnational Critical and Aesthetic Paradigm: A Study on Mozambican Literature — João Paulo Borges Coelho and Rui Knopfli
ANA MAFALDA LEITE and ELENA BRUGIONI

ABSTRACT. The Indian Ocean stands out as a transnational aesthetic paradigm, whose critical and conceptual interrelations make way for several transdisciplinary itineraries that are indispensable to (re)think the epistemological meaning of the literary representations of imperial and national narratives. By analysing the work of two prominent Mozambican authors, *Índicos Indícios* by João Paulo Borges Coelho and *A Ilha de Próspero* by Rui Knopfli, the aim of this text is to tackle the Indian Ocean as a *transnational imaginative geography* (Ghosh & Muecke, 2007) that has become crucial to (re)signify the matrices of Mozambican past, present and cultural imagination, a paradigmatic archive *in an ever-shifting set of idioms around 'tradition'* (Hofmeyr, 2007).

KEYWORDS. Indian Ocean Studies, African literatures, Mozambican literature, human ocean, archive, heterotopia.

RESUMO. O oceano Índico destaca-se como paradigma estético transnacional, cujas inter-relações críticas e conceituais abrem espaço para diversos itinerários transdisciplinares indispensáveis para (re)pensar o sentido epistemológico das representações literárias das narrativas imperiais e nacionais. Ao analisar a obra de dois destacados autores moçambicanos, *Índicos Indícios* de João Paulo Borges Coelho e *A Ilha de Próspero* de Rui Knopfli, o objetivo deste texto é abordar o Oceano Índico como uma geografia imaginativa transnacional (Ghosh & Muecke, 2007) que se tornou crucial para (re)significar as matrizes do passado, presente e imaginação cultural de Moçambique, um arquivo paradigmático num conjunto de expressões idiomáticas em constante mudança em torno da 'tradição' (Hofmeyr, 2007).

PALAVRAS-CHAVE. Estudos do Oceano Índico, literaturas africanas, literatura moçambicana, oceano humano, arquivo, heterotopia.

Islands, Theory and the Postcolonial Environment: Reading the Work of Khal Torabully
ELENA BRUGIONI and UTE FENDLER

ABSTRACT. Considering the scholarship developed within the research projects NILUS (FCT, Ref. PTDC/CPCELT/4868/2014) and Indian Ocean Aesthetic

(FAPESP grant 2016/26098-5), both in the field of Indian Ocean Studies, this article aims to address the concepts of *island* and *insularity* as strategic frameworks for (re)thinking discourses on identity within a postcolonial critical and theoretical perspective. Based on the theorization proposed by Mauritian poet Khal Torabully, namely the concepts of *coolitude* and *identité corail* (Carter & Torabully, 2002), the article presents an overview of the relationship between those two concepts and the better-known notions of *négritude* and *créolité*. The discussion presented aims to trace out new critical pathways with a view to reframing postcolonial critical discourses on identity and hybridity within the specific cultural and material context of oceanic studies, and of what has come to be defined as the postcolonial environment.

KEYWORDS. Indian Ocean Studies, insularity, Island, coolitude, negritude, creolity.

RESUMO. Considerando as pesquisas desenvolvidas no âmbito dos projetos de investigação NILUS (FCT — Ref. PTDC/CPCELT/4868/2014) e A Estética do Índico (FAPESP — Ref. 2016/26098-5) ambos situados na área de Estudos do Oceano Índico, este artigo aborda os conceitos de ilha e insularidade como marcos estratégicos para (re)significar os discursos sobre identidade numa perspetiva crítico-teórica pós-colonial. Analisando a teorização proposta pelo poeta mauriciano Khal Torabully, nomeadamente, os conceitos de *coolitude* e *identité corail* (Carter & Torabully, 2002), o artigo apresenta um panorama da relação entre esses conceitos e as noções, mais consagradas, de *négritude* e *créolité*. A discussão apresentada visa traçar novos caminhos críticos, a fim de (re)enquadrar o discurso crítico pós-colonial sobre identidade e hibridez dentro do contexto cultural e material específico dos estudos oceânicos e do que vem sendo definido como ambiente pós-colonial.

PALAVRAS-CHAVE. Estudos do Oceano Índico, insularidade, ilha, Coolitude, Negritude, Creolidade.

Combining the Uneven: Literatures of the Lusophone Indian Ocean in the Context of World-Literature — Proposal for a Theoretical Approach Applied to Mozambican Literature
MARTA BANASIAK

ABSTRACT. In recent years, new tendencies have come to light in the field of literary studies, namely when it comes to what we can call (semi-)peripheral literatures, which until recently seemed to be 'comfortably' subsumed under the postcolonial label. Over time, (semi-)peripheral literatures have attained a more mature status; in addition, technical development and globalization have significantly changed the modes and spectrum of their circulation. This has fostered new theoretical perspectives for the analysis of such literatures, and, what is more, Postcolonial Theory itself has received several critiques and begun to undergo reformulation. In view of the above, in the present essay we propose to apply the theory of world-literature (as developed mainly, but not only, by Warwick Research Collective) to the literatures of the (Lusophone) Indian Ocean. Combined with theories of Indian Ocean Studies, it proves to be a particularly interesting analytical tool for this research field. This theoretical approach is being 'tested' on modern Mozambican narrative and allows us to think this narrative in the context of different systemic alliances.

KEYWORDS. Indian Ocean Studies, world-literature, combined and uneven development, Mozambican literature.

RESUMO. Nos últimos anos, novas tendências surgiram no campo dos estudos literários, nomeadamente no que se refere ao que podemos denominar de literaturas (semi-)periféricas, que até recentemente pareciam 'confortavelmente' subsumidas sob a denominação pós-colonial. Com o tempo, as literaturas (semi-)periféricas atingiram um status mais maduro; além disso, o desenvolvimento técnico e a globalização mudaram significativamente os modos e o espectro de sua circulação. Isso tem fomentado novas perspetivas teóricas para a análise de tais literaturas e, mais ainda, a própria Teoria Pós-colonial recebeu várias críticas e começou a sofrer reformulações. Em vista do acima exposto, no presente ensaio propomos a aplicação da teoria da literatura-mundial (principalmente, mas não apenas, conforme desenvolvida pelo Warwick Research Collective) às literaturas do Oceano Índico (lusófono). Essa teoria, combinada com os Estudos do Oceano Índico, prova ser uma ferramenta analítica particularmente interessante para este campo de pesquisa. Esta abordagem teórica está a ser 'testada' na narrativa moçambicana moderna e permite-nos pensar esta narrativa no contexto de diferentes alianças sistémicas.

PALAVRAS-CHAVE. Estudos do Oceano Índico, literatura-mundial, desenvolvimento combinado e desigual, literatura moçambicana.

Literature in Transit between Goa and Mozambique: Campos Oliveira as a Pioneering Figure
ANA MAFALDA LEITE and JOANA PASSOS

ABSTRACT. In his youth, in Goa, José Pedro Silva Campos Oliveira was a regular contributor to the literary magazine *Ilustração Goana* (Goa, 1864–66), a periodical that, at the time, stood out as a standard of aesthetic refinement, attuned to the latest cultural trends. This periodical combined local creativity and cultural references with the dissemination of European literary trends. Later, while living on the Island of Mozambique, Campos Oliveira founded the magazine *Revista Africana* (1881, 1885), the first literary periodical in that country. The relevance of researching Campos Oliveira is justified by his contribution to the development of Goan literature in Portuguese, mainly his collaboration with *Ilustração Goana* and his pioneering role in creating a literary magazine in Mozambique. As his work connects literary activity in Portuguese on both margins of the Indian Ocean, we argue that Campos Oliveira was an editor and author in transit across different societies of the Indian Ocean, a diasporic subject, who stands as an exemplary figure in a transnational literary system that testifies to south/south regional dynamics and the cultural exchange of influences.

KEYWORDS. Khal Torabully, *coolitude, identité corail/coral identity*, Indian Ocean studies, postcolonial environments.

RESUMO. Em Goa, José Pedro da Silva Campos Oliveira foi assíduo colaborador da *Ilustração Goana* (Goa, 1864–66), um importante jornal literário goês que se destacou como referência de gosto estético e de atualização cultural, combinando criatividade e interesses locais com o intuito de divulgar modas europeias. Mais tarde, na Ilha de Moçambique, Campos Oliveira foi o fundador da *Revista Africana* (1881, 1885), o primeiro jornal literário desse país. O interesse particular em recuperar a figura de Campos Oliveira tornando-o objeto de um estudo mais aprofundado deve-se não só ao facto de ter deixado uma obra de relevo em Goa, sobretudo pela colaboração com a *Ilustração Goana*, mas também por ser figura pioneira na criação de uma revista literária em Moçambique. No seu todo, o legado de Campos Oliveira é testemunho da transferência de influências culturais entre Goa e Moçambique, ligando a atividade literária em língua portuguesa nas duas margens do Índico. Campos Oliveira surge assim como um autor e editor ligado à diáspora e circulação por diferentes sociedades do Índico, fazendo parte de um sistema literário transnacional, que testemunha as dinâmicas regionais sul/sul e respetivas trocas culturais.

PALAVRAS-CHAVE. Khal Torabully, *coolitude, identité corail/identidade coral*, Estudos do Oceano Índico, ambientes pós-coloniais.

The Other (Hi)Stories: Diasporic Tides of the (Lusophone) Indian Ocean in 'Skin' and 'O Outro Pé da Sereia'
KAMILA KRAKOWSKA RODRIGUES

ABSTRACT. The 2001 novel *Skin* by Margaret Mascarenhas tells a story of a young US-born and raised journalist of Goan descent who returns to her paternal homeland to overcome a personal trauma. The 2006 novel *O Outro Pé da Sereia* by Mia Couto also presents a female protagonist who returns to her hometown after years of living in almost complete solitude in a nearby village in the Zambezi region of Mozambique. In both novels, the protagonists Pagan and Mwadia need to delve into the history of the Indian Ocean slave trade to understand the tensions and fractures within their own families and the communities they belong to. By listening, reading, and narrating the two characters engage in tracing and reconstructing the silent — and silenced —

history of their families and of the free and forced migrations traversing the region for centuries. Symmetrically, *O Outro Pé* offers an intergenerational literary account of Indian Mozambicans while *Skin* portrays the virtually invisible black community in Goa. This article explores how and in what ways storytelling is a tool for remembering, re-enacting and rewriting traumatic waves of displacement, in a cathartic process in which both victims and perpetrators can be given a voice. By analysing the two novels in a mirror-like perspective within the framework of Indian Ocean Studies and Critical Archival Studies, this article addresses transnational identity building in post-imperial and postcolonial contexts in which the past seems like a haunting presence.

KEYWORDS. Slavery in the Indian Ocean, memory, storytelling, Mozambican contemporary literature, Goan contemporary literature.

RESUMO. *Skin*, o romance de Margaret Mascarenhas publicado em 2001, conta a estória duma jovem jornalista de origem goesa, nascida e crescida nos Estados Unidos, que regressa à sua casa paternal para lidar com um trauma pessoal. O elenco central d'*O Outro Pé da Sereia*, um romance de Mia Couto (2006), é também desenvolvido a partir de uma viagem de regresso — a protagonista volta à sua cidade natal após anos de vivência numa aldeia na região do Zambeze (Moçambique) em quase completa solidão. Em ambos os romances, as protagonistas Pagan e Mwadia precisam de explorar a história do tráfico negreiro no Oceano Índico para compreender as tensões e as fraturas entre os seus familiares e dentro das suas comunidades. Ouvindo, lendo e narrando, as duas personagens começam a traçar os rastos e a reconstruir a silenciosa — e silenciada — história das suas famílias e das ondas de migrações livres e forçadas que foram travessando esta região por séculos. Simetricamente, *O Outro Pé* oferece um testemunho literário intergeracional da comunidade indiana em Moçambique enquanto *Skin* representa a virtualmente invisível comunidade negra em Goa. Este artigo explora como e de que maneiras o ato de contar estórias funciona como uma ferramenta para relembrar, reatuar e reescrever as traumáticas ondas de deslocamento, num processo catártico no qual tanto as vítimas como os culpados podem ter voz. Analisando os dois romances numa perspetiva comparada dentro dos enquadramentos teóricos dos Estudos do Oceano Índico e dos Estudos Críticos Arquivísticos, o artigo aborda a formação da identidade transnacional num contexto pós-imperial e pós-colonial no qual o passado parece assombrar o presente.

PALAVRAS-CHAVE. Escravidão no Oceano Índico, narrativa, literatura moçambicana contemporânea, literatura goesa contemporânea.

Enchanted Things to Narrate the Oceans: João Paulo Borges Coelho and Luís Cardoso
JESSICA FALCONI

ABSTRACT. This article stems from the research developed within the NILUS project and, in particular, it fits into the research strand that explored the role of material culture and materiality in contemporary narratives of the Lusophone Indian Ocean. The article focuses on the short story 'O Pano Encantado' [The Enchanted Cloth] (2005) by João Paulo Borges Coelho and on the novel *Requiem para o Navegador Solitário* [Requiem for the Solitary Sailor] (2007) by Luís Cardoso — two narratives set in insular spaces, the small Island of Mozambique and the island of Timor, respectively. It aims to validate the hypothesis according to which calling upon material culture and materiality offers a way of narrating and remembering (in) the Indian Ocean from different margins of its area of influence.

KEYWORDS. Indian Ocean, material culture, memory, João Paulo Borges Coelho, Luís Cardoso.

RESUMO. Este artigo resulta da pesquisa desenvolvida no âmbito do projeto NILUS, inserindo-se, em particular, na linha de investigação que pretendeu explorar o papel da cultura material e da materialidade nas narrativas contemporâneas do Oceano Índico lusófono. O artigo foca o conto 'O pano encantado' (2005) de João Paulo Borges Coelho e o romance *Requiem para o navegador solitário* (2007) de Luís Cardoso, isto é, duas narrativas que se situam em espaços insulares — a pequena Ilha de Moçambique e a ilha de Timor, respetivamente. O artigo pretende validar a hipótese segundo a qual convocar a cultura material e a materialidade é uma forma de narrar e lembrar (n)o Oceano Índico a partir de distintas margens da sua área de influência.

PALAVRAS-CHAVE. Oceano Índico, cultura material, memória, João Paulo Borges Coelho, Luís Cardoso.

East Timorese Literary Narratives (Twenty-First Century): Indian Ocean Crossings and Littoral Encounters
GIULIA SPINUZZA

ABSTRACT. We aim to analyse the book *Requiem para o Navegador Solitário* (2007) by Luís Cardoso considering the maritime elements that emerge in the novel and combining Indian Ocean Studies with Gender Studies. Pointing to the East Timorese imagery and the perspective of the female protagonist, we will focus on the elements related to the coast of the island, such as the shore, the sea, the ships, the sailors, and the interconnection with other islands and territories during the colonial period. We will analyse the link between the existential trajectory of Catarina, the female protagonist of the novel, the history of East Timor and Indian Ocean crossings. This text, written in Portuguese by a Timorese author, portrays the complex history of this territory during World War II and offers a unique perspective on Timorese history.

KEYWORDS. Indian Ocean Studies, Gender Studies, island, coast, sea, literature from East Timor, Luís Cardoso.

RESUMO. Pretendemos analisar o livro *Requiem para o Navegador Solitário* (2007) de Luís Cardoso a partir dos elementos marítimos que emergem neste romance e através de uma articulação dos Estudos do Oceano Índico com os Estudos de Género. Ao apontar para o imaginário timorense e para a perspetiva da protagonista feminina, iremos focar os elementos relacionados com a costa da ilha, como o litoral, o mar, os navios, os marinheiros e a interligação com outras ilhas e territórios ao longo do período colonial. Analisaremos a ligação entre a trajetória existencial de Catarina, protagonista feminina do romance, a história do Timor Leste e as travessias do Oceano Índico. Este texto, escrito em língua portuguesa por um autor timorense, retrata a complexa história deste território durante a Segunda Guerra Mundial e oferece uma perspetiva única sobre a história de Timor Leste.

PALAVRAS-CHAVE. Estudos do Oceano Índico, Estudos de Género, ilha, litoral, mar, literatura timorense, Luís Cardoso.